ACHIEVING

Peak Performance in Tennis

Helen K Emms

lıp

A PRACTICAL GUIDE

to developing your mind and energy system for winning

ACHIEVING

Peak Performance
in Tennis

Helen K Emms

First published in 2008 by:

Live It Publishing
27 Old Gloucester Road
London, United Kingdom.
WC1N 3AX
www.liveitpublishing.com

ISBN 978-1-906954-00-0 (pbk)

To my mum
with love and gratitude

Contents

Acknowledgements

To all the people I have worked with and learned from, without whom this book would not have been published, since it is they who have provided the source material for this book. They are the foundation from which the academic knowledge I have learned has been applied. Their successes are indicative of their own personal desires to achieve their peak performance and highest potential. Thank you for having the courage to pursue your dreams.

To my academic teachers and personal mentors, for shaping my understanding, skills and practical application of the science around peak performance. May the flow of knowledge, life long learning and personal development continue for us all.

To my family and friends for your support, guidance, and love. Thank you for being there. I love you all.

Foreword

At Gosling we aim to offer every player the opportunity to succeed by developing to their full competitive tennis potential which can only occur by developing a player's mental, physical, tactical and technical capabilities.

Helen has worked with Gosling coaches, players and parents in the mental aspect of player performance to develop values, mindsets, an action focus and techniques that have enabled players to maximise their strengths in their physical, tactical and technical skills. Helen's work has dramatically improved the quality of the training sessions, the speed of learning and most importantly the players' results. If you want to fulfil your competitive performance on and off the court I thoroughly recommend this book.

Matt Willcocks, Tennis Director

Gosling High Performance Centre

Author's Note

This book has been written on the back of many years of academic studies in various disciplines related to human development, including psychology, energy psychology and sports psychology and an equal number of years developing players, coaches and parents to help them better utilise their mind and energy system to achieve their highest potential. Every single one of us is capable of achieving peak performance; our highest potential. I use these two terms interchangeably since to me they are one and the same thing. What stops players from achieving their peak performance, or highest potential, is often fear. Fear presents and manifests in a multitude of different ways that you are unlikely to have considered before now. In order to overcome fear it is necessary to understand what it means to be human. This book is therefore about understanding what it means to be you, no matter what your current level of performance, and how to use the power of your mind and spirit ("chi" energy) to achieve your peak performance in tennis.

Throughout this book I have given you real coaching advice and activities to overcome your human barriers to success. The advice I pass on to you here is the same advice that my clients have used to transform their performance. You will find that as you work through one aspect of your development so other things will come to the fore. This is the natural process of development and one that I encourage you to embrace.

You may find yourself dipping into individual sections and chapters that appeal at any one time. That is fine and will help to guide you on specific aspects of your game. But I also urge you to read the first two sections to get a real feel for the major influences in your game, many of which you may not have been aware of before now. Some of the things you read about here, you may not feel you have any control over. That may or may not be true and I urge you to always look for where you can take control rather than in the first instance assuming that you can't take control.

The main purpose of this book is to help you to become more aware of yourself; the influence of your mind and spirit, and teach you how to deal with anything that stops you achieving your highest potential. So that you can free yourself up to go and get your dream, improve your game and feel great.

In the first section of this book, we take a look at your brain and mind and some of the tricks your mind can play on you. Throughout this section of the book you will become aware of how your mind works. You will learn how you make sense of the world and how key human thinking patterns can significantly impact your performance. You will come to appreciate that your mind and your tennis is not exactly as it would first appear. You will develop a different perspective on your reality and begin to look at your game with new fresh eyes. Your thinking will be challenged and as a result you may experience a feeling of discomfort, which will be a sign that you are about to improve.

As you will come to realise during the first section, nothing you think is "absolutely true" in so far as all things can and do change. Your thinking can change, your understanding can change and your results can change. Scientific understanding changes with new learning, which means many things we thought were true some years ago we now know are not true! The same is true for how you, through your mind and energy system, interpret your game; your interpretation of your game is not absolutely true. That also means that what you read in this book is not true in an absolute sense either! It is, however, what players experience and therefore it is true for them. You must make your own judgment as you read and apply what is written. I will say though, that it is only through the application of what is written that change can take place in your game.

The second section is all about your energetic self and the energetic influences on your tennis. This may be something you have not considered before now, but it is useful to recognise that your chi energy system is the source of your personal power, your spirit and your life. Without this energy you would be dead. It is that simple. Yet, many players do not realise the power they have. As a player your energetic power is often misdirected, which means you don't get the best out of your game. In this section you will learn to recognise the impact of your chi energy and how to raise your awareness to destructive patterns so that you can make changes to support your tennis development. To not be aware of how your energy works for you is like playing tennis with a blindfold on and one arm tied behind your back; it's very dark and something is missing! During this section, if you have not studied your energetic self before, there may be some information that you find really challenging to relate to. I urge you to simply do the exercises and find out for yourself. Learn what works best for you, which is unlikely to be the same for other players. Begin to really and truly appreciate "you" and what you need to do to be your best.

In the third section we look at a wide range of aspects of the mental game of tennis and you will learn how to apply your mind and energy to achieve winning results more often. You may already be familiar with some of the headings, which are more often seen in traditional texts, such as focus and concentration, confidence, motivation, imagery and goal setting. You can of course read individual chapters if that is what appeals to you, but in doing this you may find that you need to refer to other supporting chapters. This is because every aspect of the human psyche is interlinked with other aspects within your psyche.

For example, you may be interested in developing your confidence and in reading about how to do that in the chapter on confidence you will also be drawn to read about your memory and self-evaluation, and you may find that you want to go back to the chapter in the first section on interpreting your tennis experience. Remember, everything you do, think, or feel is linked to something else; nothing happens in isolation. One thing contributes to another. Your job is to recognise the contributing factors to the mental and energetic aspects of your game and deal with them so that you can free yourself up to play better tennis more often.

In order to make the book more readable and accessible I have put very few academic references within the text. Also, there may perhaps be some topics that are of more interest to you than others, such that you would like further information on them. You can visit my website where you will find a wide range of academic references and recommended reading:

www.AchievingPeakPerformanceInTennis.co.uk

You will also have access to a bank of practical resources for your own personal tennis development, such as a confidence programme to follow, feedback sheets, further information on each of the chapters in the third section, and a coaching question and answer forum for your personal use. The coaching forum is there for you to pose questions that arise out of your application of the content of this book, and any additional coaching advice that you need to develop your mind and energy system to achieve peak performance. This resource based website has a wealth of information to support you to continue your personal journey to transform your game.

Finally, at the back of this book you will find a glossary of key terms and key concepts for those of you who are not familiar with the terminology and particularly within the context in which it is written.

I hope you enjoy your journey as much as I have enjoyed writing this for you. If you really want it... then go for it!

SECTION
One

Tricks
of the Mind

Introduction

The idea that your mind and spirit (energy) have a significant impact on your performance and that they are directly linked to the achievement of your results in tennis is not new. There is a whole field of psychology now that exists to support the development of peak performance. The development of your mind and spirit (chi energy) should be key elements in any comprehensive training programme in the modern game. Whilst the mental aspects of performance are sometimes covered within such programmes, the energetic influences are largely ignored, at best summed up in the terms "player attitude" or "emotion". But, your "spirit" and "energetic self" is much more than these things and has a significant impact on your ability to achieve your peak performance.

It is of course not always easy to quantify the contribution of your mind and spirit to your improvements since the impact of both can sometimes be quite intangible. Yet in a competitive environment where technical and physical performances can be very close, your mind and spirit will be the difference that makes the difference. However, in this Western world of performance measurement and rewards based on results, it can make it more difficult for players and institutions to fully appreciate and evaluate the value of mental and energy skills training.

It is also the case the some people still feel a little sceptical whether they can train and change their mind and energy, perhaps seeing things as fixed, which of course is not true. Sadly, it is still also the case that players work harder on all other aspects of their training and spend much less time on their mind, even though they admit that their errors are of a mental cause. Maybe it's because mental training can be tough, maybe it's because it can be considered expensive? Following the coaching guidance herein will make your mental skills training the best value for money you can find.

What is true is that, if you are embarking on mental game training, you need to take a leap of faith and believe in your ability to use, change and direct your mind and energy and you need to take action. Of course, for those already converted, training your mind and spirit really is a no-brainer!

In this first section of the book I will talk about some of the foundations for the remaining two sections; our mind and how it works and some of the realities and not so "real" aspects of our mind and brain. These foundations are necessary so that you will have a base line appreciation for the power house that sits between your ears and how it works very hard to support you even against the odds, and sometimes in ways you are not expecting! The first chapter focuses on why your mind and spirit matter in the game of tennis. You will appreciate the difference between your brain as a structure with functions and your mind, which is a whole lot more than the structure. You will become aware of the impact of your brain and mind on your performance and results in tennis. Then you will be taken on a deeper journey into your psyche; discover your own reality and explore how you interpret your experiences. You will see how you can change your interpretation to support what you want to achieve. We look at the notion of perception or deception and how your mind will deceive you if it is in its best interest to do so at the time, and what it means to become aware of your mental performance.

We will explore the power of truth, winning and maybe, because they are three concepts that have a significant impact on your attitude in the game. You will raise your awareness of your natural tendency to generalise your experiences and predict your results, to the extent that you can even predetermine your game and the outcome, through your thinking and energy patterns. You will identify what it really means to have a pessimistic or optimistic style of thinking, the damage done through simple judgments and how to shift your perspective on your performance to achieve a more positive outlook.

A most important chapter is that on responsibility, causality and results where you are encouraged and taught how to be open and honest with yourself and take responsibility for your outcomes. You need to be able to do this without feeling like a failure so you can become more personally powerful in the game. Finally, in this section, we look at one of the most destructive of human dilemmas; the problem of needing to be right and the impact of your desire to be right on your ability to progress and make changes (whether technical or otherwise) in your performance.

1

Mind Matters &
So Does Your Spirit

I wonder if you have ever really considered the impact of your mind on your performance and your results? Ask yourself, how do you measure the impact of trust on your performance? Your mind is the key that can transform your game, but you have to take appropriate action for change to happen and before you can do that, it helps if you know a bit about how your mind and spirit works.

To explain how you use your mind and spirit (also referred to as energy or energy system) we will follow some simple and relatable concepts. Of course, this simple approach cannot possibly capture the full complexity of your mind and spirit, and in my view our mind and spirit is so vast and intangible that nothing can. The concepts that I will share with you, some of which you may be familiar with, will be appropriate for you to be able to relate to what you do with your mind and energy in tennis and what you need to do to achieve peak performance.

Once you have read this section, you will begin to see clearly the relationship between what happens in your external tennis experience and how you interpret and subsequently respond to it. You will also become familiar with some of the natural human psychological barriers that make achieving peak performance more difficult. With this understanding it is possible for you to begin to identify what and how to change in order to achieve better and more consistent results, have more fun and also feel good no matter what happens!

Before we explore the detail a word of caution is necessary! If this is the first book you have read on all this stuff about mind and energy then some of what you read may appear a bit daunting. You may feel you have to monitor every thought or action you take. Or, you may be someone who has tried to change things in the past and not really achieved much success. Often people struggle when they try to change their mental approach, because they try and change too much too quickly or they experience internal resistance to change. Please don't rush and don't start monitoring every thought you have as that is more likely to confuse you and render you frozen to the spot. When you begin the process of changing your mental and energetic approach to your game you must do so gently and with respect for yourself and particularly with respect for what you have achieved to date.

Throughout this book you will be guided along your own personal journey to improve your game and consequently your life. Please be gentle on yourself and remember that you have done your best to get where you are now. If you had known how to do things differently before you would have done so, but you didn't know and therefore you couldn't do it differently, could you?

Your mind is the key that can transform your game, but you have to take appropriate action for change to happen and before you can do that you need to know how your mind works. Don't try and change lots of things at once and don't start monitoring every thought you have. Be gentle on yourself and remember that you have done your best to get where you are now. With new information you can achieve your peak performance.

BRAIN POWER

You will already be aware that your brain and mind are extremely powerful and complex. Please be aware that your brain and mind are different. If you have taken time to think about it before now, you may be in awe of the amazing capacity that your brain has. It is said that we have more neurological connections in our brain than there are grains of sand on the planet... that's a lot of neurological connections and for those of you who want to see the number, it looks like this, $(10^{10})^{11}$ or:
100,000,000,000,000,000,000,000,000,000,000,000,000,00
0,000,000,000,000,000,000,000,000,000,000,000,000,000,
000,000,000,000,000,000,000. That's a lot of brain cells!

Scientists have also discovered that the capacity of our brain far exceeds what we actually use; in fact we only use about 10% of our brain capacity, which means there is a lot more that we could be doing with our brain. Our brain is often described as the central computer system of our body. Therefore, you could think of your brain as the "structure" of what lies between your ears. In computer terms, think of your brain as the hardware and your mind as the software. Both are necessary and both require programming for them to work effectively together.

Your brain is split into two halves. There is a left and right side of your brain, each of which has different functions. However, they are linked so that they both can influence each other. The left side is generally associated with the following:

➢ logical, rational, analytical, and structured thinking,

➢ critical evaluation,

➢ linear processing,

➢ numerical functioning,

➢ strategy and planning,

➢ voluntary control,

➢ thinking of future and past events,

➢ determination, effort, trying, and

➢ from an energetic perspective it is described as "male".

The right side of your brain is associated with:

➢ creativity,

➢ language,

➢ intuition,

- ➢ multiprocessing,
- ➢ automatic movements,
- ➢ feel, touch, rhythm,
- ➢ visualisation,
- ➢ present moment,
- ➢ modelling,
- ➢ body language,
- ➢ effortlessness and
- ➢ from an energetic perspective is described as "female".

I need to clarify here that the terms male and female do not mean that men operate left brain and women right brain, but instead refers to the type of "energy" involved, of which men and women have both types!

Our brain has a left and right side each with different functions and both are connected so that they interact with each other. Some of the functions of the left brain are: logical, rational, critical, evaluative, past and future focused and determination and effort. Some of the functions of the right side are: creative, language, intuition, feel, touch, rhythm, present moment and effortlessness. Using both sides of your brain effectively is a key to achieving peak performance.

There are also three levels of brain development that influence how you respond to external events, and therefore they will have an impact on your attitude and behaviour in your game. The oldest part of your brain is called your "reptilian brain" and according to scientists this part of your brain is responsible for your instinctive and more animalistic characteristics. Your "fight or flight" response, which is your natural and automatic response to danger, is controlled by this part of your brain. Some human characteristics that are controlled by this part of your brain are:

> ➤ cold bloodedness, with no empathy with the victims of your actions,
> ➤ territoriality and a desire to control,
> ➤ obsession with hierarchical structures of power,
> ➤ aggression and the idea that winners take all, and
> ➤ the desire to win at any cost.

A player operating through these characteristics may be limited in achieving their peak performance, since there is little higher level brain functioning. It is important however, to first become aware that some of your instinctive behaviours have a biological drive. They were not built into your brain for the purpose of playing tennis. Therefore it is important that you recognise you may need to change behaviours that feel quite instinctive and natural to you in order to be the best that you can be.

The focus of the reptilian brain is survival and its main motivation is fear. It is connected to your brain stem, which starts at the top of your spine, and receives your immediate response to a situation. Because the reptilian brain is responsible for your "fight or flight" response, as a player you can easily respond with an instinctive fear response rather than through emotional balance and reasoned thought. Your reptilian brain also responds and reacts more powerfully to visual stimulus rather than verbal instructions, which may explain why some players respond so badly to seeing themselves making mistakes and no amount of verbal encouragement touches them! Your desire for excess also comes from your reptilian brain. That desire for more, which is a natural human function, has a necessary place in your development as a player and yet it can also be quite destructive too. One of the positive functions that stems from your reptilian brain functioning, in the context of tennis, is the adherence to ritualistic behaviours. The world's best players all use routines and rituals to create stability and focus in their performance. We will explore the role of such rituals and routines in Section 3. For now, just be aware that your desire for routine and ritual is a positive function of your reptilian brain and your desire to win at all costs may be costing you!

The second structure to develop in the course of our development as human beings was our mammalian brain. It contains the organs that control our automatic functions, such as digestion, body fluids and blood pressure. It is also responsible for the storage of experience based memories and for your experienced based recognition of danger. It is also responsible for the fact that you respond according to past events and have some conscious feeling about those events. The feeling of guilt after an event is a function of the mammalian brain structure.

Whereas your reptilian brain is controlled purely by instinct, your mammalian brain is consciously aware of you in relation to the environment. This means you act with consideration for others and you have feelings in relation to your actions.

The third structure to develop in us was our neo-cortex. The neo-cortex is, essentially, the left and right brain structures that were mentioned earlier. Through this part of your brain you carry out more "conscious thinking", i.e. thoughts you are aware of, rationalising, understanding, organising and processing of your experiences. The activities of the left and right hemispheres are a function of the neocortex. Every structure in your brain; reptilian, mammalian and neocortex, in a normally functioning person, is linked and therefore in communication with every other part of your brain, and your body. Although, individual players may use various parts of their brain more or less dominantly which may lead to an imbalance and therefore present difficulties for the achievement of peak performance.

When a player responds with rage, or if they are "manipulating" the game to ensure they win (in the junior game cheating is a common problem), it is potentially their reptilian, survival based brain that they are allowing to dominate. In order to overcome reptilian functioning, young players must be taught to follow their higher brain functions (mammalian and neo-cortex). In other words they must become more aware of their impact on other players, the impact cheating has on them after the event and the need to rationalise their desire to "win at all costs". As mentioned earlier, your reptilian brain functioning can be used powerfully in tennis through adherence to routines and rituals.

There are three levels of brain development that influence how you respond to external events; reptilian, mammalian and neocortex. Reptilian functioning is very instinctive and animalistic. It is responsible for your "fight or flight" response which is your natural response to danger. It is also associated with animalistic aggression and a "winning at all costs" response. It is the part of your brain that is used to develop rituals and routines in tennis. Mammalian brain functioning controls your automatic functions and is responsible for your memories and how you feel about them. Your neocortex is responsible for your thinking and rationalising processes. Achieving peak performance means using each of these parts of your brain to their best effect and not allowing instinctive negative responses to dominate your game.

Of course the question remains, how can you control this brain functioning if it is a natural biologically driven part of you? That is a good question and you may instinctively feel that you cannot control it. However, it is important to think of your brain functioning more in terms of "tendencies" rather than absolutes. If you think something cannot be changed then you won't make any effort to change it and you will be stuck with it because you think it cannot be changed. If you think it can be changed you will make an effort to change it and therefore you can change.

Having a tendency towards a particular behavioural response is not the same as doing that behaviour. With time and practice you can change your behavioural responses to any given situation. To begin this process of change however, you first need to raise your awareness to what you do, raise your awareness to what feels natural and instinctive in you and then create a space between the instinct arising and your subsequent behavioural response. The space I am referring to is called time. Give yourself time before you respond to an instinctive experience.

To change your natural behavioural responses you first need to create a space between your desire to respond and your actual response. Give yourself time before you respond so that you can begin to respond differently than you would do if you just went with your instincts.

MIND POWER

Now, you are probably already aware that your mind is much more than your brain. Whether you have thought about it already or not, it would be incorrect to think of your mind as controlling your body, as if communicating in one direction only. It is more useful to think of your mind and body as an intricate communication system. Your internal communication system happens using what is called electromagnetic and neuro-chemical signals, which are transmitted between your brain and body and between your body and brain. It is now thought that these neuro-chemicals bathe every cell of our body and therefore our mind and body are in fact one. You can think of this electrochemical messaging system between your mind and body as being your internal electrical circuit, like the signal between two telephones. You cannot see it, but you know it is there because there is someone talking to you on the other end of the line!

To help you relate to your mind, it is easier to think about it as if it has two different levels, your "conscious mind" and your "unconscious mind" (sometimes called sub-conscious mind). Think of your mind as an iceberg (see Fig 1. below), where the bit sticking out of the water, the tip of the iceberg, is your "conscious mind" and the main bit of the iceberg lying under the water is your "unconscious mind".

Fig 1. The Conscious and Unconscious Mind

You can see by this representation that your "conscious mind" is very small in comparison with your "unconscious mind". Your "conscious mind" is best understood as whatever you are thinking about, or aware of, at any moment in time. Let me show you how to experience the difference between your "conscious" and "unconscious" minds right now. As you are sat reading this book you may not have been aware (until I mention it) of the feeling of your hands touching the book, or your feet in your shoes (unless you are in some pain). But as I mention these things to you and you focus your attention on them, you are using your "conscious mind" to do so. You were still experiencing your hands on the book and your feet in your shoes (assuming you are wearing shoes) before I asked you to bring them into your "conscious awareness", but you were still experiencing them, and everything else, in your "unconscious" at the time.

Your "conscious mind" is also linked with some left brain functioning, such as analytical and critical thinking, evaluation and linear processing. Your "unconscious mind" then is everything else that you know or and have experienced, which is stored and therefore not in your conscious thoughts at that the time. Your "unconscious mind" is often linked with right brain functioning, such as creativity, intuition and emotion.

Now, you need to be aware that your unconscious storage of everything you have ever experienced is also thought to be held in your body as well as your mind! So your mind and body are totally connected. Your body can therefore be a fantastic indicator of what is going on in your mind, which means that you can learn a lot from tuning in to your body and how it feels and responds to situations.

Fortunately, you can influence what you have stored in your "unconscious mind" so that you can get rid of any negative emotionally charged experiences. To do this you have to first become "aware" of the relationship between your mind, energy and body. Something you will be doing throughout the following chapters and in doing so you will begin the process of change to improve your results and the enjoyment of your game.

Let's look at another example to help you appreciate how your "conscious" and "unconscious" minds operate together, to manage your experiences. If I ask you to recall your telephone number, you would be able to say it out loud to me (unless you have a memory block at the time of me asking you). Where was it before you recalled it to me? It was stored in your unconscious mind, which may feel like a sort of "outer space". Your unconscious mind may even feel as if it is outside of you. So, to be able to tell me your number you would bring your telephone number from your unconscious, where it is stored in some neurological/energetic form into your own conscious mind, where you can speak it in language.

This means that essentially everything you experience, whether you are aware of it or not, is having an impact on your body and therefore your results. And please think broadly here, because we are not just talking about your results in tennis, we are talking about your results in life. Making something conscious, in other words becoming aware of it, is the first step in the cycle of learning. It is necessary for us to identify our bad habits so we can change them to achieve peak performance. Your brain and mind play a powerful role in your openness to learning, whether that is mental skills, technical skills or tactical skills in tennis. Resistance to learning will always hold you back from achieving your highest potential. Openness to learning is an essential quality for any player wishing to achieve their peak performance in the game.

To complicate matters even further, the thoughts you have are not always "conscious" thoughts. In other words, you may have thoughts that you are not aware of, which are stored in your unconscious mind and I will call these your "beliefs". Recognising that you are not always aware of the thoughts that are influencing your behaviour is helpful since it will encourage you to investigate yourself in more detail and through your learning about yourself you will improve your performance. If you believe that you only function at a conscious level you are likely to close down your options as you will not be aware of your total contribution to the game. What you think and believe will have a major and significant impact on your performance and your results. Your "beliefs" and unconscious thoughts may only be made obvious by your performance and behavioural patterns. Becoming aware of these patterns is critical in identifying your deeper barriers to peak performance.

Electromagnetic signals and neuro-chemicals are the communication process by which information is sent between your mind and body and vice versa. Your mind and body are totally connected and therefore what goes on in your mind strongly influences your body. Your conscious mind is best understood as what you are thinking or aware of at any moment in time and your unconscious mind is everything else that you experience and you are not aware of at the time. You may not be consciously aware of all your thoughts. Unconscious thoughts such as beliefs can be identified through your behaviour.

SPIRIT POWER

So, what do we mean by your "spirit" and how does that fit in with becoming a great tennis player? Many people have an idea of spirit. We hear terms such as "fighting spirit", "free spirit", "the spirit of a champion", "in good spirit", and I am sure you will have your own interpretation of what they all mean. It may help to think of your "spirit" as an energetic aspect of your mind. Within the book when I have referred to your "energy" or "chi" this also includes your "spirit". Here are some other definitions of spirit:

> ➢ excellent attitude in terms of courage, intent, etc.; determination: That's the spirit!

> ➢ feelings or mood with regard to exaltation or depression: low spirits; good spirits, high spirits.

> ➢ the soul or heart as the seat of feelings or sentiments: a man of broken spirit.

> ➢ conscious, incorporeal being, as opposed to matter: the world of spirit.

> ➢ the incorporeal part of humans: present in spirit though absent in body.

> ➢ the principle of conscious life; the vital principle in humans, animating the body or mediating between body and soul.

I have watched many players who have been present in their body, but not present in "spirit". When you play at your best, mind, body and "spirit" are all present at the same time. The loss of "spirit" may happen fairly early into the game and is often, and probably not surprisingly, stimulated by losing or the feeling that you are going to lose! You will know when you see "spirit", as it is that essence in a player that means they stand out amongst other players. They may not always win the game, but their "spirit" remains strong even in the face of defeat. Your "spirit" is your energy. It is the energetic aspect of each of us that is both within and beyond our body and which strongly influences our physical actions. However, I want to differentiate here between that form of spirit, which is driven by the need to prove something as compared to what I consider to be the more positive and healthy form of spirit, which is driven by the desire to experience something and develop oneself. Healthy spirit is the energetic part of us that is simply engaged in the pleasure of being and experiencing our game and life, with all the challenges that brings.

The spirit that I recommend players develop is this latter form of "healthy spirit", because it is directly linked to the development of your self-confidence, self-esteem/self-worth and it gets results too! You will see this type of spirit in professional players; in their determination and drive to be the best they can be, simply because they love to improve themselves, for their own sense of satisfaction and fulfilment.

This is very different from the form of spirit that is found in many amateur players, which is driven by more reptilian brain functioning such as; the need to feel powerful, to feel better than others, the need to dominate and control or win at all costs. This form of spirit, which I shall also label "ego" based spirit may get results. However, I have never seen "ego" based spirit lead to a strong sense of self-esteem, fulfilment or happiness. The main reason for this, which is discussed in Section 2, is that your ego can never be totally satisfied. This means "ego" based spirit is not sustainable over time. Whilst it is not possible, nor is it desirable to play totally without ego spirit, you do need to strive for a balance in this energy in order to achieve your peak performance.

The best players in the world are strongly driven by their own sense of achievement and they play with that healthy form of spirit which is linked to developing a strong sense of self-confidence, self-esteem and personal fulfilment. Rarely are they trying to prove how good they are to others, although of course, this may be an additional by product of their success.

One way to identify which form of spirit you are playing with is to look at your main motivations for playing. Are they for external factors such as rewards, accolades, status, or social approval or are they more intrinsic (inside you), such as the desire to improve and be personally enhanced through your experience of playing tennis? Those of you who are driven predominantly by external forces will of course enjoy the game when you are winning, but you may struggle to get pleasure from playing the game when your winning streak comes to an end. As you develop your motivation and become more intrinsically driven, you will begin to enjoy the game more and become less frustrated by the errors you make, and you will more often have mind, body and spirit present at the same time for the game!

Think of your "spirit" as an energetic part of your mind and body, which includes your moods and attitude. You need to play tennis with your mind, body and spirit in the same place at the same time. To achieve your peak performance you need to learn to have a strong spirit even in the face of defeat and this means developing a more healthy spirit. Healthy spirit is developed when your desire to play tennis is driven by more internal factors, such as the desire to improve and be challenged, the desire to develop and see how good you can be. Ego spirit can be very destructive to your game and your self-confidence. Ego spirit is where you are driven to play more for the results, status, social approval and your need to feel powerful, than the pleasure of playing. You cannot play without ego, but you can learn to balance these driving forces so that you build confidence.

2

Interpreting Your Tennis Experience

On many occasions as a Peak Performance Coach I have watched performances at all levels. I have spoken to players, coaches and parents after the match and more often than not, the interpretation each gives of the game will differ. Yet, we have just watched the same game! It is of course commonly appreciated that two people can witness the same event and have different interpretations, but this can cause much distress between player and coach and more particularly between player and parent! So, let's understand how we interpret what happens on the outside of us – our tennis experience.

Maybe you have wondered why some players do really well and others don't? Why some players can talk about their game positively no matter what happened and why some players will always beat themselves up even when they have performed well? Even within families, where there is genetic similarity, two people can see the same event and describe it very differently. I wonder how many times coaches, parents and players have had a very different perspective of a performance? This difference in perspectives can be a source of much irritation and distress, and may even end up as a battle of who is right and who is wrong. Developing your "player perception" in a healthy way is of key importance to you achieving peak performance. And as any coach, parent and player knows, telling a player that wasn't what happened, doesn't work that well!

The way in which we process our experiences in life and consequently our game is shown in the communication diagram at Fig 2. below, which comes from the discipline called Neuro-Linguistic Programming (NLP). NLP is the art and science of how people experience the world and how they communicate with themselves and others. Essentially, it is about how you use your mind to create your results and therefore how you can create the results you want through specific ways of thinking and behaving. NLP was started by Richard Bandler and John Grinder around 1975 by modelling highly successful people; experts in various disciplines, so if you prefer, you can think of it as the science of using your mind to create excellence!

As I describe how you process and make sense of the world you will begin to understand a bit more about how you personally interpret your experiences. With this understanding you will become aware of how you perceive your game. Knowing how you perceive your experiences may not in and of itself change your perception (although that is possible), but it will help all parties (players, coaches and parents) appreciate that the different perceptions are all correct", since they are simply as they were experienced and interpreted at the time by each person concerned.

Players wanting to improve must become aware of how they perceive themselves and their performance and learn to become more open to changing their perception. Whilst you remain unconsciously blind to what is happening, you will be resistant to change. You may deny that anything is wrong until a long way down the line, which if you have high aspirations for your game could be too late.

You may also be someone who fails to see the great things you are doing, and therefore you judge yourself too harshly. This is simply your perception and worth changing. Be aware that when you are changing your perception you may need to trick your mind before you really begin to see things differently. In other words you may have to accept the perception of others to be correct. Of course you only want to do this if it helps you to become a better player.

We will later explore each of the filters through which we perceive our experiences so that you can become familiar with how to make changes to your perception. But first, let me explain how you perceive and make sense of your experiences and therefore your game.

EXPERIENCING REALITY

You will see on the left hand side of Fig.2 that we have an external event. The external event is clearly something that happens outside of us, such as; the ball going in the net, your opponent giving a bad line call, the weather conditions, parents and coaches saying something. Even though you may have taken some action such as hitting the ball, the actual experience of that event is happening outside of you. Have you ever really stopped to consider how you experience the event inside of you? You can only experience the outside event through your 5 senses: sight, sound, touch, taste, smell. What you experience through your senses you will of course label, with words; your language.

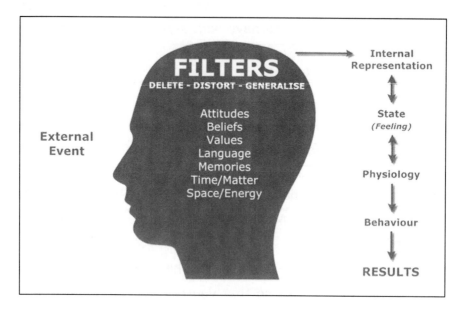

Fig 2. Communicating and Making Sense of Our Experiences

According to scientists, what you are actually experiencing outside of you is some 2 million bits of information, which is bombarding your senses every second. Now, clearly if you tried to process 2 million bits of information every second you would go crazy so you have built in natural ways of filtering the sensory information you are receiving from the external world. Those filters are called "distortion", "deletion" and "generalisation". An example of you distorting your experience will be when your coach gives you positive feedback about your game and you say to yourself that it wasn't that good. You are distorting what your coach says to suit your own opinion. An example of deleting your experience is when you don't see something you are doing well and you only see the bad things. You delete the good stuff! Generalising your experience is when you say that you always play badly at a specific venue or on a specific surface. You are generalising one or two events to the whole thing.

So we will all distort, delete and/or generalise our external experiences in order to be able to process them in our minds. In fact we distort, delete and generalize from the 2 million bits of information coming into our senses down to only about 134 bits. This means that just 0.0067% of the sensory data we experience we actually use to form our internal representation of any event! Your internal representation is therefore your mental image of the external experience; it is your own personal reality.

What then influences your filtering process? Each of us has a unique set of sub-filters, which are your values, beliefs, language, memories, attitudes, and your concept of time, matter, space and energy. It is through the operation of these sub-filters that you give meaning to your experience. As an example, if you are a player who holds a belief that honesty is good and someone cheats you, you will perceive their cheating as dishonest and you will respond accordingly. The player who doesn't see cheating as dishonest will have a different response from you. I hope by now you can begin to see how we can all see things differently and how it is possible for one person to "see" what another person cannot.

Now, the content of your sub-filters was, originally, installed in you by your parents and other significant people, your culture and societal norms. These people and their rules in life will have had a strong influence on you when you were growing up. What is important to recognize here is that what you have stored in your sub-filters can be changed. The rules that you were taught may not be appropriate for you now and they may not support you in achieving your highest potential. This means that if what you are doing, thinking, feeling and how you are interpreting your game is not helpful to you, you should make every effort to change it.

It is useful to think of your sub-filter content as your personal programming. How you have been programmed and how you continue to programme yourself influences your response to situations you experience, how you make sense of your game and how you quickly you develop your performance. You can see how easy it is for you to judge your performance in accordance with the content of your filters. Coaches and parents should also be aware here that you will judge a game based on the content of your filters. In order to judge your performance differently you will have to commit to looking at your game with new eyes. In this way you can override your habitual thinking and begin the process of reprogramming your mind so you can achieve greater success in your game. Overriding your habitual thinking requires that you do something differently. You need to start by actively looking for positive things in your game, no matter how small they may be.

Remember, you experience something external to you through your 5 senses. You then filter these sensory signals through your sub-filters (beliefs, values, etc.) from 2 million bits down to 134 bits. The 134 bits that you focus on determines your perception of reality. The content of your sub-filters influences how you give meaning to your external experience and this together generates your feelings and emotions and an internal physiological response. This in turn determines your behaviour and therefore your results.

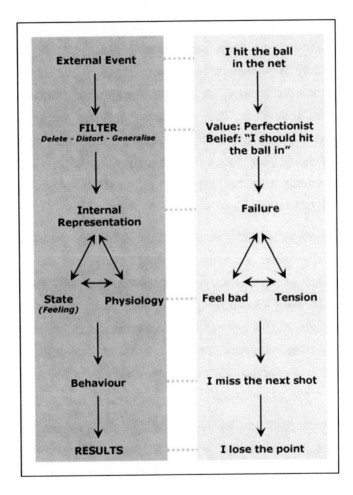

Fig 3. The Process

So, let's see that process in the context of tennis, which is presented in the flow diagram above at Fig 3. If a player believes it is important to be perfect, which is a common problem in tennis, they may hold a belief such as "If I play perfectly I will win". They might also have memories of playing perfect shots and winning points. They may also have a value around perfectionism, which means that being perfect is important to them. These are all the rules that the player is holding as "true" in their mind, the breaking of which can feel very painful to them. So when you as a perfectionist player make a mistake, and especially a simple error, your "rules" have been broken. This causes you to feel threatened and your "fight or flight" response is activated. This in turn creates a negative feeling (because in your mind you are not being successful) and tension, which is physiological response. This then leads to a behavioural response, which may be missing further shots, steering the ball or losing depth control and spin.

Excessive activation of your fight or flight response, which you will experience as a physiological state, results from your interpretation of something as a threat to you and leads to over activation in your nervous system. This over activation in your system results in the tightening of your muscles, mental tension, emotional over-reaction and a lack of rational, cognitive functioning... a recipe for disaster that can become a self-sustaining cycle of destruction!

I am sure that you can easily see, from how we process our experiences, how it is that we can all have different views of the same event. Not every player will run the same rules about perfectionism and therefore, different players will react differently to making errors. We are all individually correct in our perceptions and technically there is no absolute reality. The only reality that exists is the one that you perceive through your senses, which makes it very real for you. All you need to ask yourself is this; is my perception of my game supporting me achieving my highest potential or is it holding me back? As a player, to take control of your game, you first need to learn to change the content of your filters and recognise when you are distorting, generalising and deleting information in a way that is destructive to your performance.

Throughout the third section of this book you will be coached in more detail how to identify all the mental aspects of your tennis that you can change to improve your performance. As you follow the guidance it will also help you to change your perception of your game. To be successful you simply have to want to play better tennis, want to win more often and be committed to working at changing your mind in ways that support the achievement of your peak performance. You need to be prepared to do that bit extra that the other players aren't doing. Then you will have a competitive edge.

You create your own reality based on how you perceive your experiences. You can filter what you experience in the external world in any way you choose and to change your perception of your game requires you to look at what you are doing differently. The content of your sub-filters, which was installed in your early years, will give meaning to your experience, which will also create an emotional and physiological response. These responses lead to your behaviour and your results. If you don't like your results you can either change your behaviour or you can change how you filter your experiences by challenging the content of your filters and replacing it with something that contributes to you achieving peak performance.

3

Perception
or Deception

As we saw in the previous chapter, you perceive the world
through your senses and based on the content of your sub-filters
you will distort, generalise and delete information to come up
with an internal representation, which will have meaning to you.
Your internal representation will be unique to you as no-one else
will filter exactly the same way as you. The content of your sub-
filters is very strongly influenced during your early years (birth to
about 7 years) by parents and significant care givers. Between
the ages of 7 and 14 heroes, icons, pop stars and other such
influences have a strong impact on your filters. From the ages of
14 through 21 peer pressure has the most dominant effect on
your filters, which for those parents reading will explain some of
the difficulties you experience through the adolescent period as
your dearest son or daughter would appear to go in completely
the opposite direction to your teaching!

These phases of individual development have clear implications for the development of a tennis player, not least because the influence of parents and coaches is strongest in the early years.

Young players, particularly, are more likely to need external validation of their performance. At a very young age, and into teens, the need for external validation is common as youngsters are trying to work out where they fit in the hierarchy of life. In my experience, the external validation provided by tennis coaches and parents is both common and can be a problem for longer term player development. A player who needs constant external validation of their performance and improvement may struggle to take responsibility for their own performance and will remain dependent on their coach/parents and others who they work with.

Players who have a strong need for external validation are also likely to change their coach or training location when things aren't going well for them.

If you are a player who needs constant reinforcement that you are doing the right thing, you will likely feel great when your coach gives you that reinforcement, but in essence you are building your self-confidence based on an external source – your coach! Whilst it is always nice to receive good feedback you should not rely on this alone to feel good about your game. To rely on others to feel good about your game is a vulnerable source of confidence and creates dependency.

Players need to, and should be encouraged to, develop a positive self-evaluation so as to develop a more intrinsic appreciation of their performance. To do this requires a careful balance; that a player be supported in their self-evaluation, even though their perception may not be the same as the coach's. It also requires that the player raise their awareness to their game, which may mean the coach has to challenge their perception. It helps if this is done in a positive way by pointing out how what the player has done mentally has contributed to the outcome they achieved in the game.

It goes without saying that the process of becoming aware is essential to your development in tennis. If you remain unaware of what you are doing, how you are creating your results and why you respond the way you do, you will be deceiving yourself and limiting your success. Yet many players have a poor level of awareness and particularly when it comes to what they are doing with their mind and energy. This is in part due to the emphasis on technical and tactical instruction that has dominated the teaching of the game over many years. It is also due to the fear that people still hold fear when it comes to training their mind and energy; fears such as manipulation and brainwashing are common. Without realising it, the only person who is brainwashing you is you!

When I ask a player to become aware of what they are doing, either in training or whilst competing, they will always respond with how their forehand was working or the fact that they missed a couple of drive volleys. They may even be able to give me technical reasons as to why these errors have occurred, but most players' appreciation of their mental and energetic contribution to their errors is very limited if is even recognised at all. It is interesting that in tennis we talk about and measure "unforced errors", which means that the error cannot be attributed to the opponent hitting a good shot. However, from a mental perspective the error was forced, by the player himself not his opponent! Something you did caused you to make the enforced error; it may have been technical, but more often than not it has mental and energetic causes.

Unforced errors may be attributed by the player to losing concentration or feeling under pressure, but often errors are made when not under pressure, especially in the amateur and junior player's game. So even when a player recognises that they have lost concentration when they were just about to play a "winning" shot, their awareness isn't with the route cause of the problem. The real question is; "what happened that caused you to stop concentrating in that moment?" Very often when a player messes up an easy shot or a "winner" the answer to this question is that they thought they had won the point, before they hit the shot. They were too focused on the outcome (winning the point) than the process (executing the shot).

Therefore, the process of becoming truly aware involves honest introspection, which can be somewhat frightening, but is also liberating and empowering. It is frightening because the act of owning up to your own deficiencies can make you feel vulnerable and inadequate and the idea of change scares most players to death (even though acceptance of change is very important in the development of your game). And yet, by the very nature of going through the process of self-evaluation and introspection, you also become liberated and empowered because you are more in control of what you are doing.

Let me explain. You are unaware of how your game is failing you when you use "excuses" such as; "the other player raised their game". This is a common reason given by players when their game takes a dip during a match. You might notice it as a change in momentum if you were watching. Whilst as a player you remain unaware of your contribution to your dip in performance during the game you are losing your personal power; losing control over the game. You are also deceiving yourself. The other player has power over you. They have your power because they can play on your weakness, and you put your results down to what they are doing rather than what you are doing.

As soon as you raise your awareness to the fact that it is your concentration or your lack of discipline in your routines, or even your forehand that is not holding up, then, as painful as it might be to admit this fact, you can take action to rectify the situation. Even knowing your forehand isn't great means you can play a different tactical game than you would do without that awareness.

Awareness is the key to change, which is why many players will deny they need to make changes in their game until their performance becomes so bad that they are forced to take notice. They are simply not aware and this lack of awareness perpetuates their self-deception.

You need to develop a strong internal validation system rather than just relying on others to tell you are doing well. Awareness is the key to change. Taking back your control and personal power in the game means becoming aware of your mental contribution to your errors and then taking action to change it.

Awareness of your mental errors is much harder to detect, especially if you are not aware that you have control over such things as emotions, concentration, confidence etc. Technical faults are more easily identified, in part because they can be seen by others.

Self deception is most often not a conscious activity. In other words, many players will not realise that they are deceiving themselves. If a player is aware at a conscious level, and still not being honest with themselves, then they are more likely to be in denial. They know but they are denying it.

Deception on the other hand is to some extent a trick of your perception and I believe, as with denial, it serves to protect you in some way. So, if a player feels uncomfortable about making changes to their game, because they fear their results won't be as good (there is always some risk with change) they will not want to see how their game is not working.

Therefore, when they select the bits of information in the environment that form their internal representation, they will actually distort or delete the information accordingly. They will see things as being fine, until such time as the evidence really stacks up against them and they can no longer deny it.

An example of this is seen particularly with young naturally talented players, who achieve great results up to a point in their young careers. They are naturally talented, perhaps because they are bigger and stronger as a young junior than their peers, but at some point as they develop other players catch them up or over take them. At some point they become aware that they have to take serious action or they become unable to compete. This can be a painful wake up call for young players who have achieved great results with little effort and perhaps no mental training at all. They have done well in the past, why should they change now? Players may even leave the game at this point in their development as they become less successful at competing and their dreams feel unattainable.

The process of raising your awareness is best done with evidence rather than just through different perspectives. A coach's or parent's perception of the game may carry little weight when the player perceives their game as successful. Objective evidence is very helpful for coaches and players as it depersonalises the experience. It also means the coach is not putting their own bias into the process. The player gets the real data on their game and even though, as we have found coaching players, some will still argue that it didn't happen, the evidence soon becomes clear. Tools such as charting and plotting patterns of play and video feedback are ideal for highlighting and depersonalising feedback. Of course, coach and parent can still impart their own bias when talking through objective feedback!

Again, let's be clear here: the raising of awareness can be a painful process for some players as they can feel very vulnerable and insecure. But once a player is working in this way, they can achieve their full potential, because they will continue to evaluate their performance in a positive and constructive manner. With a higher level of awareness a player will be better able to develop their training programme to meet their needs in the game.

It is important you accept that to develop your mental approach requires you to operate at a higher level of self awareness than you would in normal do day to day living. It means looking at your performance and the patterns you tend to run. For example, do you regularly mess up the winning shot when you have an easy shot to play? Do you often double fault or lose points when you are 40:15 up in the game? Do you lose more points following a simple error? Where what you are doing works, that's great carry on. But when you are running patterns that don't get you the results you want, you need to look for the underlying mental patterns that create your behaviours and work to change them.

Let me give you an example to further illustrate the link between a physical response and the mental cause. When working with a player and their coach, the player was in the process of developing a more attacking style of play. The coach had noticed that whenever the player made a mistake they tended to automatically revert to a defensive game style. This was a consistent pattern of behaviour which had an underlying psychological cause. The player was not aware that they adopted this pattern of reverting to a defensive style when training and performing. The coach raised the pattern of play to the awareness of the player. The player became aware that they were unconsciously operating with a fear of making mistakes that resulted in "default" behaviour, of reverting to a defensive style of play following a mistake. Now, for months the player had been working on being more attacking, but kept reverting to a defensive style when competing, which was frustrating. She was both unaware of the pattern of play and, more importantly, the reason for her defensive behaviour. When she became aware that this pattern was linked to her underlying fear of making mistakes she was able to immediately over-ride her natural tendency and play a more attacking game. Knowing that it was her fear that was creating the pattern she was better able to take action. Prior to that she wasn't aware enough to take any action and simply pointing out the pattern of play had not stopped it happening in matches or training.

Deception is a natural process that we adopt which serves as a protection for things that we don't want to become aware of, or feel we can't handle. It is particularly important to begin to raise your awareness to the massive contribution of your mind and energy to your game. You control what you do with your mind and you control how you use your energy, so you can now choose to use this wonderful tool to your advantage and move out of the shadow of deception and into the light of personal honesty and openness to change. That's how you create and use your personal power in the game. That's how you begin to achieve your highest potential.

4

Truth, Winning &
The Power of 'Maybe'

Many players I have worked with, and especially younger players, struggle with interpreting their game and developing their perception because of what they believe to be absolutely true. True and truth are different.

Something can be true but not a truth, so for example it is true that "I lost the game to John" last week. However it is not a truth that "I always lose to John". In other words, a truth is something that holds true universally and always. You cannot know that you will always lose to John therefore it is not an absolute truth. You can of course predict that you will always lose to John, and if you predict it you are likely to achieve it, but it is still not a truth. It cannot be a truth because it cannot be proven.

Many players talk about their game and their results as if they are a truth; that it is always that way, rather than simply recognising that it was true at that specific moment in time. Such over generalisations are of course a factor of a faulty perception. It is also a negative projection which is more common amongst amateur players and inevitably leads to underachievement.

When a player generalises in this way they are taking an event in time, such as losing to John, and projecting that every time they play John they lose to him. Of course this perception becomes stronger and eventually becomes an accepted norm, a belief. It becomes their absolute reality. The loss that takes place on the court will be influenced strongly by the perception that the player takes onto the court. If you start out with a belief that you always lose you can easily create that outcome.

The truth of the matter is simply this, just because I have lost to John before doesn't mean that I will lose to him today. Therefore, when players say that they cannot beat someone, what they really mean is that they haven't beaten them yet. The power of your language cannot be underestimated here and if a player says they cannot beat someone, they are effectively predicting that fact, which means it is more likely to manifest as true for them. It is therefore important that players use language that keeps their options open, such as using the word "yet".

You must begin to recognise, through your language, whether you are projecting or talking about your tennis in terms that would suggest an absolute truth rather than just true at that point in time. Now you may be thinking that it would be great to project successful outcomes all the time, and this is indeed how many players are taught to think. After all you wouldn't want to be saying to yourself "I haven't lost, yet!" What I am suggesting to you here is to use the word "yet" to break down negative projections. I will address the downsides of positive thinking later.

Of course, what we believe to be true is often based on past experiences, commonly held convictions, myths and superstitions within and about the game. Players can easily use past experiences as a measure of their ability and since memories are more easily recalled if they are linked to a strong emotional response, the tendency of players to recall negative past experiences and generalise those to future events is easy to see. But it doesn't make it true for future events (until after the event).

Sadly, we more often see players recall past negative events than past positive events. There will be many reasons for a player recalling past negative events in their immediate evaluation of their game, one of which is linked to our innate desire to be better than others. This may sound counter intuitive, but our drive to be better than others can lead us to identify our failures and measure ourselves against others. We not only have a biological drive to be superior (driven by our ego and reptilian brain) but we also live in a Western society that measures failure more than it measures success; we have a stronger tendency to focus on problems, with a view to solving them, than we do have a focus on solutions. It is also easier for us to identify what we didn't do well as often this has more emotion linked to it and may have resulted in us not achieving our goal: to win!

Back in cave man times, if man had not been successful in finding and attaining food he would have to change his strategy and in order to do that he would need to know what was not working. The same is true as a tennis player, with a slight difference in that your life doesn't depend on it, although with some players this is not always obvious!

Finally, we have in the UK, a strange, rather outdated and negative attitude when it comes to outwardly expressing our success, often captured in such terms as "over-confidence" and "arrogance", which I will address in Section 3. Underplaying our success is common, destructive to achieving peak performance and undermines self-esteem and self-confidence.

Psychologists often talk about pessimistic and optimistic thinking styles. A player with a pessimistic style will see their failures as permanent, generalised and their own fault and they see their successes as non-permanent, specific to that event and lucky. But this style of thinking can and should be changed to achieve better results and for you to enjoy the game more. You can choose whether you see something as permanent or not. This pattern of recalling negative performances is very common and almost "cult like" in tennis and it begins from the very start, but it isn't true. Even in social tennis, players are prone to immediately reflecting on what they haven't done well. We are far more comfortable talking about what we did badly and what we need to improve on than we are talking about what we did really well. We are operating well within our comfort zones when we are being critical of ourselves and that makes it more difficult for us to change.

Perfectionists often struggle with this pattern of negative thinking too. Perfectionists are highly critical of their performance and consequently experience high levels of associated negative feelings. Don't get me wrong here, it is necessary to evaluate your performance and to identify what you need to do to improve, however it is quite something else to beat yourself up for things you didn't do so well and not celebrate those things you have done well. Perfectionism is discussed further in Section 3, but if this applies to you, start now by becoming more balanced in your self appraisal, recognise there is no absolute truth and develop a healthy awareness that supports your tennis development.

To be a great tennis player it is essential to reverse this negative pattern of evaluation and reflect on positive past events and generalise those positive performances to future events; what Psychologists call an "optimistic" style of thinking.

Become aware that whatever happens in your game is not absolutely true for you. In other words, it can change. Just because you played badly yesterday doesn't mean you will today. Generalise your positive experiences and see your negative experiences as random. Use the word "yet" if you haven't beaten someone before. Focus more on your successes than your failures.

Of course, what makes it difficult for us to predict a positive outcome, is that negative results are much easier to achieve than positive ones and we wouldn't want to predict something unless we are fairly certain it can be achieved. Many people believe there is a greater certainty in predicting the negative and of course that is because it is much easier to achieve. But, it is also true that players are more likely to achieve what they predict (whether that is success or failure). I will talk about this in more detail when I address our energy system in Section 2 and how we attract the results we get.

Many players, and especially young players, go into a match having assessed their chances of winning (usually solely based on the rating of their opponent) and depending on their prediction, will play accordingly. Now, when I say that they have assessed their chances of winning, this may not be a conscious activity on their part; in other words, they may not be aware that they have done this. If you are a coach or parent you can begin to notice whether they have made this kind of assessment in their language and behaviour.

As a player, you need to raise your awareness to your thoughts and feelings about your fellow competitor to notice whether you have made an assessment of probability about your chances of winning. Suffice it to say, whatever prediction you make, you will work hard to make it come true, even when it isn't what you really want.

This type of predictive thinking creates more problems than it solves, since tennis is a game that involves considerable uncertainty, unfairness and unpredictability. For now, simply remember, "Where your attention goes your energy flows". What you give your energy and attention to you are more likely to create. Failure is easy to create, it is the soft option, especially if you are one set down and losing the second set 3-1. Success on the other hand requires that you overcome your psychological baggage, which will be linked to many factors including fear of failure, needing to be right and feeling insecure.

Players may also continue to evaluate themselves during the game, making decisions about whether to run for the ball or not, how good a particular shot was, whether they are being successful or not, and whether they can keep it going in the next set. All of these predictions are a distraction and result in underperformance.

You may be wondering why we would predict failure and yet have a fear of failure? Here's what I have noticed. If we predict that we are not going to do well today, we don't put in as much effort as we would do if we predicted we could do well. So if we don't put the effort in, we can mitigate the feelings of failure because we can change our interpretation of what happened. It's as if, in the back of our mind we know that we didn't really try and because we didn't try we can't truly be held accountable for our results. I wasn't really there in the game in terms of my mind body and spirit, therefore it wasn't really my fault. Failure is easy to predict and if you do predict it, it is very easy to manifest. From the perspective of developing confidence and self-esteem this is a flawed thinking strategy that can only lead to further feelings of failure and dissatisfaction.

However, since no player wants to go into a game expecting to lose or predicting that they will lose, even though unconsciously they may be thinking this way, many players try to develop, and are taught to develop, a strong positive attitude about winning. So, many players end up thinking that to be successful means they have to focus on winning. But the truth is that focusing on winning doesn't create winning results. Why? One reason is this. A focus on winning easily becomes a focus on not losing! When a player evaluates and calculates their likely success before they play, based on past experiences, ratings, rankings and other such flawed information, strange things can happen. The following scenarios, which I have regularly seen are examples of what can happen in a game:

> ➢ If the player has worked out that it is going to be a tough match and then they start playing and losing a few games, even though they are focusing on winning, what happens is their dominating thoughts will actually switch to "not losing". This often happens when ratings are close.

> ➢ If the player is playing someone who they calculated they should beat and they start losing, even though in their minds they feel they are focusing on trying to win, their dominating thoughts will again switch to not losing. They will struggle to win and under-perform.

> ➢ If the player gets ahead in a game they think they should win, they can easily think they have won and switch off too early, which then allows the other player into the game, which subsequently causes them again to focus on not losing.

> ➢ If the player is playing someone better than them and they start winning, strange things can happen! Because they never expected to win they can unconsciously sabotage their performance. An example of this behaviour in action was with a player who did exactly that. She had match point against a much better rated player and during the match point her opponent hit the ball clearly

long (by about 4 inches). She didn't call it out and went on to lose the match. After the match she could not work out why she hadn't called the ball out, even though she had clearly seen it was out. She admitted that she never thought she was going to win the match and so, without her realising it she had worked hard to manifest her result!

So focusing on "winning" can easily switch to a focus on "not losing". And focusing on not losing is very different from focusing on winning. When you focus on not losing you are more likely to create exactly what you don't want; losing. This is because your unconscious mind doesn't process negative images. Whatever we think about we create as an image in our mind. Whether it is phrased as a negative or not makes no difference. So for example, if you say to yourself "don't hit the ball in the net", what image immediately pops into your mind? The image of your ball going into the net, right? So, now you have given your attention to the ball going into the net and effectively given your body, including your muscles, the message to hit the ball into the net. So, please don't be surprised (pun intended) when you hit your ball in the net. Remember, where your attention goes your energy flows.

Your judgment of certainty, as to whether you can beat a player is based on a number of factors including; past experiences, which are in the past, training performances (past) and an assessment of ratings or rankings, which are also a reflection of past performance. Of course the past is all you have upon which you can make judgments, but remember the past is not a reflection of the future. So just because you played well yesterday doesn't mean that you will play well today, equally, just because you didn't play well yesterday doesn't mean you will play badly today. But sadly, players undermine their potential when they buy into these fixed "past based" ways of thinking. To not make a judgment is to be in the present moment. Being in the present moment is where you want to be when playing tennis.

What players often fail to realise is that they actually have nothing to lose in any game they play. Of course this is not their perception because most players measure their success solely on their wins, ratings and rankings, which are essentially ego based measures. Such measures are also the cause of more failures than successes.

Whatever you predict in your game you are likely to achieve because you will put the appropriate level of effort into the game to achieve your prediction. Predicting failure is easier than predicting success. Positive thinking only works when you stay focused on what you want to achieve. If you are focused on winning, it is easy for your attention to change to not losing instead and if you focus on not losing you are more likely to achieve losing. Play tennis with a desire to win and a maybe I will maybe I won't attitude. Then work hard to do your best in the game. Avoid predictions of success or failure based on past based data and instead see what happens when you get on court.

The ideal thinking strategy for a player is to recognise that maybe they will win, maybe they won't. This attitude of "maybe" should always be accompanied with a desire to win and play well, since that is why you enjoy the game. You also need to focus on the process of tennis rather than the outcome (but more about that in Section 3). So, a winning attitude is in part about having a desire to win and do well. Then to say, "maybe I will win, maybe I won't", "let's play" and "just see what happens", and to then focus totally on the process of tennis, the implementation of which will create your results. This is a far healthier and more balanced approach to playing the game that will take the pressure off and free you up to play your best tennis more often. If you feel you cannot do this then you can use the remaining chapters to find out why you can't and let go. You need to free yourself up from unhelpful thought patterns so that you can play your best tennis.

5

Responsibility, Causality & Results

I have already touched on the tricky subject of players taking responsibility for their performance, which on first thought many players may believe that they are already doing this, but I have to say from my experience, the majority are not.

Knowing where the boundaries of responsibility lie in the game is the start. I have seen many players blame their coaches, their training programme, parents and others who are supporting them for their failures. Players sack coaches when things aren't going well for them, but really we need to understand the dynamics of the mind that are at play here.

It is probably a truth that everyone struggles to take full responsibility for their actions in this life. Why? Simply, fear. Fear that you are not good enough, fear of being wrong, fear of failure. It doesn't matter what the fear is about, it is fear. If you take responsibility for yourself then you have to hold your hand up at the end of the day, and for most players this is hard to do. But to not take responsibility will limit your ability to achieve your best. The player who needs something to blame will always find reasons and excuses as to why they didn't do well today, and in doing so will potentially undermine their self-confidence and self-esteem. Of course the reasons and excuses can be very good and even believable. But it is still a form of self deception that will hinder your development. When you take responsibility for your game you will progress more quickly, achieve your best results more often, have higher self-confidence and self-esteem and a greater sense of self fulfilment.

Newtonian based science and philosophy states that for everything that happens in the world there is something that caused it. The same is true for you and your performance; for every outcome that happens in your game there will be a cause or causes that contributed to that outcome. The question is: What are the causes? Here in lies the problem. Many players attribute the causes of what happened during their game to something outside of themselves; their opponent, the weather, the court, line calls, the crowd.

Taking responsibility is not about blaming yourself. It is about recognising your contribution to your results rather than putting your results down to something outside of you. Many coaches are encouraged to teach players to "let go" of their negative outcomes during a match and take pleasure out of their positive results. This is very important in helping a player preserve and build their confidence. However, letting go of the negative results during a match is very different from disowning negative results.

Disowning your input to negative results is to blame something outside of yourself for the fact that you didn't do as well as you could have. Such lack of ownership and blame can at best keep you blind or ignorant to what is going on in your performance and at worst cause you to experience inner conflict, because deep down inside you know when you have not performed well. Disowning your play is a way of subtly disowning yourself and this strategy will negatively impact your self-confidence.

Because you know deep down inside when you are not performing as well as you want to, if you don't take ownership of your contribution to your performance, you are in fact denying the truth in that moment. Whilst this may not seem important on the face of it, when performing competitively if you are not aware of how you are causing your negative results during the game it is easy to become frustrated by the outcome rather than address the causes. Taking responsibility does not mean beating yourself up for your outcomes, since this is also destructive to achieving peak performance. Of course it is not possible to say exactly what the long-term impact of not taking responsibility for your performance could have, since the impact is felt by the player inside themselves, but most commonly, confidence and self belief will be seriously eroded.

Some players I have worked with at first struggled with the idea that they need to take responsibility for their contribution when, for example, they have been given a bad line call. But let's look at that scenario in more detail. Yes, if you are given an incorrect line call you have been wronged. In the professional game there are lines judges to try to ensure that bad line calls don't happen, although even they get it wrong from time to time and so players in some tournaments are now able to challenge the decisions of lines judges. But in the amateur game, and more specifically junior tennis, this luxury doesn't exist.

So as an amateur player there is very little that you can do to challenge the line call. Some players will ask their opponent if they are sure, but the rules at this point in time are clear. The decision lies with the player making the call on their side of the court. Even if an umpire is called, rarely if ever will they counter this rule and therefore, if you are on the receiving end of a bad line call you cannot change the fact that the ball has been called out, but you have several choices as to how to respond. For example, (and this is the bit players struggle with because it doesn't seem fair) you can take responsibility for the fact that you hit the ball so close to the line that it gave the other player the chance to call it out.

I am not saying don't hit tight margins (although for the most part it is not necessary to hit the ball tight to the line to win the point), but what I am saying is if you are playing against a player who gives you consistently poor line calls (and there are a good number of them in the junior game), then you can take some action to not allow them the opportunity. You can hit bigger margins. A player who changes their game in this way is taking responsibility for their game and doing whatever it takes to get the best result that they can at the time.

Tennis is not fair and tennis players don't always play fairly or call the ball fairly, but if you allow your opponent to wind you up because of their line calling, you are the only person who is likely to suffer. You cannot change what happened but you do have choices as to how you respond and you would be best choosing a response that helps your game than a choosing a response that doesn't.

Bad line calls usually end in frustration and anger or other negative emotions, which, unless a player has been trained to direct their energy appropriately, will most likely result in more mistakes being made and deterioration in performance. More often than not the person challenging the call will suffer, and yet the reason for their suffering is the fact that they feel wronged; that they have been treated unfairly. Tennis is not fair and people don't always play fairly, but holding on to that sense of having been "cheated" doesn't help your performance.

Learning to accept the decision and take action to prevent the player having the opportunity to give you another bad call is a more healthy and positive response that will keep you in the game longer.

Tennis is of course a sport that involves another player at the other side of the court, so it is very easy to attribute what went wrong to what the other player did very well and therefore neglecting your own contribution to your failure. Often players will talk about the other person "upping" their game as a reason for them losing. I have heard this comment on many occasions and when investigated further it is clear that the other player "upping" their game was directly linked to an action on the part of the losing player.

Younger players particularly struggle with the idea that they contributed to the other person upping their game because they are not aware of the relationship between what they do in their mind and what impact that has on their performance. Very often a young player in a winning position can lose a match because they have "switched off" in some way. They may then attribute their loss to the other player raising their game rather than acknowledging that they had switched off. One of the reasons players switch off is because they are results or winning focused rather than performance or objective focused.

When a player is winning focused and they are ahead in the game it is easy for them to lose concentration; they will make errors where they were previously hitting winners. They will move more slowly around the court and be more easily distracted by external factors such as crowds or parents/coaches. As a result of the player lowering their mental input to the game the other player has an opening, which if they take it can influence the momentum of the game.

In order to keep the momentum in your favour you need to remain totally focused on your performance objectives, irrespective of the score and outcome of your play. For many players this is a tough ask. After all the game of tennis is all about results right? Well maybe! The results you get are always the outcome of a number of factors: your actions, (physical, tactical, technical and mental) the actions of your opponent, the line judges, the weather etc.

When you take responsibility for your game and recognise what you are doing that is causing your outcomes, you will be focusing more on your performance objectives than on the result itself.

Of course you can never guarantee your result because of the other influences in the game. You can only influence the result through your contribution. It's the same as baking a cake, where if you put all ingredients in as it says in the recipe and cook it at the right temperature for the right length of time you will get the cake you expected. In tennis, you cannot guarantee your results in quite the same way. You may put in all the right ingredients on the day, but the other guy's ingredients may be stronger!

The point is that you need to focus your energy on putting in the right ingredients irrespective of the score at any point in the game. That is what it means to adopt a performance focus.

Taking responsibility for your game means not blaming things outside of you for your results and it also means not blaming yourself too. When you don't take responsibility for your game you undermine your confidence and self-esteem. Taking responsibility means looking at how you caused your results and changing the things that don't help you. Remember your results are a function of a number of factors, some of which you have no control over. Take responsibility for what you can control and let go of the things you cannot control, even if you feel cheated or wronged. Do whatever it takes for you to be in the best emotional state possible to play well. Focusing on what you are doing that is causing your results means you will be more focused on your objectives than on the result itself. And remember, there are no guarantees in the game. You can play your best and still lose.

It is safe to assume that the majority of players will be results focused unless they have trained in a performance focus. This is because the game is based on results; the player with the best results wins the tournament, and for many players their results are also their only measure of performance success. It takes some consistent effort to focus on performance objectives during the game and especially when under pressure. You will discover more on setting objectives and achieving a performance focus in Section 3. For now, become aware of how you are contributing to your results, whether good or bad, and take responsibility by recognising and accepting your input to your game rather than blaming something outside of yourself. And do that without beating yourself up. A tough ask for many players, but the rewards are worth it.

6

The Problem of Needing to Be Right

I have already touched on the idea that as humans we have a strong need to be right. It is said that being right is more important to us than being loved! I don't know whether this is true, but what I do know is that there is a very powerful driver in most people to need to be right. Of course there are good reasons for this; our need for security and safety, our need to feel powerful and our need to feel confident. If I am right then I can feel secure in that knowledge, powerful and confident. The problem arises when we are not right; on being found to be wrong we can easily feel insecure, powerless and a lack of confidence. Players with a strong need to be right struggle with a number of mental game techniques since mental game training involves taking certain actions when there is a strong possibility that you might get it wrong!

An example of the impact of needing to be right is in a player's use of visual imagery. Tennis players are often encouraged to use multi-sensory imagery to; rehearse their shots going as they want them to, imagining their perfect game, and to control their emotional state, etc. Yet often players can struggle to commit to doing imagery work, even though using multi-sensory imagery has been proven to significantly enhance performance.

Unfortunately, if a player cannot imagine themselves performing successfully they are unlikely to achieve success. So as an example, if you hold a strong need to be right and you face a player who could beat you and you believe that you are likely to lose you may struggle to use mental imagery effectively to rehearse success against that player. However, by holding the image in your mind that you are unlikely to win, you are using imagery to rehearse failure. Then when you play and lose you will at least be able to say that you were right; saying "I knew I wouldn't beat her". I have seen this strategy with a number of players including one player who couldn't see himself serving successfully. All he could do was imagine his serve going long and sure enough he was able to hit is serve long with remarkable accuracy. So it wasn't that his imagery was letting him down, on the contrary, his imagery was working very well for him, getting him exactly the result he was imagining. But he really struggled to imagine the serve he wanted because when he imagined that good serve and it didn't happen he felt even more let down than imagining serving long and achieving it!

There are two points here that players would do well to remember. The first is that if you struggle to imagine yourself performing successfully against a player, check that you are not just needing to predict success. Ask yourself, "do I really think I can win this game?" And "am I prepared to put in the effort to do so?" If the answer is no you may struggle to imagine yourself being successful. The second point is that imagining success doesn't guarantee that it will happen. What it does mean is you give yourself the best opportunity to play in a way that can lead to success. Your body and mind are linked because of the neuro-chemical messages that are sent between your mind and body. So what you imagine in your mind, whether good or bad, sends signals to the muscles and micro muscles in your body, which then translates your mental image into physical action.

If you have a strong need to be right you can easily limit your progress and development since you will not want to step outside of your comfort zone and if you do you will be more likely to predict failure so as to be right and stay comfortable.

The pessimistic style I described earlier is more likely to be aligned with a player's need to be right. Pessimism is easier to be right about than optimism. Failure is much easier to be right about than success. To get the best out of your game, you need to drop your need to be right, which may also result in you dropping your need to prove yourself. All of a sudden, you will find yourself playing because you enjoy the game and you will take more enjoyment out of the challenge of the game. The need to be right and the need to prove yourself are both ego based forces which create more problems for a player than they do in helping a player. When we let go of our ego we are free to explore and push our boundaries and develop to our highest potential. We will explore our destructive ego in Section 2. For now just raise your awareness and ask yourself, is your resistance based on your need to be right? Remember it is okay to get it wrong and it is necessary for you to predict success if that is what you want to achieve.

Needing to be right is very destructive to your game, your ability to learn and your personal development. It can stop you from seeing yourself as successful and it can prevent you from adopting an optimistic thinking style. Accepting that it is okay to be wrong and make mistakes is necessary to achieve peak performance.

SECTION
Two

Energetic
Influences

Introduction

The source of your power as a player lies in your energy system. Now, by energy system here, I actually mean something beyond what you may naturally think of as your energy system. Most players are aware of their energy system in more physical terms, such as their body's use of ATP, aerobic and anaerobic functioning. In this section, when I talk about your energy system, I am referring to your subtle energy system that is the source of all life. This is energy that you cannot necessarily see, unless you are trained, and it is independent of your nervous system. Nonetheless, this energy influences your physical, emotional and cognitive functioning. This source energy is referred to as "Chi" "Qi" or "Ki" and it is your life force.

We are all energetic beings and by that I mean we are all energy transformers. We turn what we eat into energy (of the physical nature), our thoughts are energy (of the chi nature) and our feelings are energy (of both physical and chi). Energy or chi is the difference between being alive and dead! With this source energy we can achieve and without it we cannot. With lots of chi energy we can feel in "high spirits" and with less energy we can feel in "low spirits". But have you ever considered the energetic impact of your thoughts and feelings on your performance, the injuries you incur, the stamina you have and the results you get?

In this section you will explore some of the key energetic influences on your tennis that you may or not be aware of. Some of these energetic influences are driven by your source (chi) energy; others are influence by both your physical and chi energy systems. It is not important to know which energy system is involved, it is important to recognise that you are being affected by something you may be unable to see. You will most certainly have experienced the outcome or consequences of these energies even if you didn't fully appreciate how specifically it was happening within you! To achieve your peak performance in tennis you want to be able to optimise the influence of your chi energy on your performance.

In the first chapter you will learn about the source of your personal power; that is your own subtle energy system and how your chi energy influences your results. Each of the energy centres in the body, known as chakras, is talked through to give you an indication of their influence and the impact of blockages in your chi energy. We then look at the law of attraction and the notion that you attract through your thoughts and emotions the results you want. The law of attraction is interesting in the sense that where you direct your thoughts your energy goes and where your energy goes impacts your results. When players direct their attention and energy ineffectively they get poorer results. You will come to fully understand what it means to focus on what you really want to achieve in your game so that you can perform at a consistently higher standard. We then look at why positive thinking can be scary and how to overcome that small fact! Players are often told to think positively but without realising what you are actually doing it can be very difficult for some players to do consistently. You will then look at the significant and real idea of what it means when you are being true to yourself in the following chapter. The reason this is important is that being true to yourself is the key to achieving high levels of self-esteem and self-confidence. You will learn about what it means to be true to yourself and how to start doing it right away? We then look at the problem with emotions, levels of arousal and how to handle your emotions in a way that is both healthy and supporting your game. Emotional control is critical for peak performance for many reasons and not least because it affects your concentration and focus. This is followed by a chapter on channelling anger and then on unfreezing fear, for those who particularly struggle with such emotions. Then there is a chapter on our destructive ego which will give you a new perspective on the way your mind impacts your performance and even your desire for the game. Your ego is a dominant force that is neither good nor bad, but when you are operating through your ego energy, you will create very different outcomes, confidence is harder to build through ego and results can be very erratic. This is followed by the final chapter of the section; the energetic forces of nature. The universally recognised, archetypal energy influences that you are unlikely to have considered before but which strongly impact your ability to achieve your peak performance and your highest potential.

7

The Source
Of Your Power

You have already seen how your mind and body are connected, the fact that neuro-chemicals and neurotransmitters are responsible for delivering messages throughout every cell of your body. Your energy system is inextricably linked with the functioning of your neurotransmitters and neuro-chemicals in your body. In this section of the book, you are going to take a deeper look at your subtle energy system, known as "chi" and understand how you can begin to manage your chi energy more effectively to create the results you want.

Our body has a number of energy centres known as chakras, and energy channels known as meridians, which control the flow of chi energy around, and in and out of, our body. Think of the chakras and meridians as being the same as your veins and arteries. They provide the energetic nutrients that your body needs. Your energy meridians follow specific paths through your body and feed every cell of you. The idea of your chakras and meridians, how they work and the problems that can arise when there are blockages in your energy system stems from Japanese and Chinese Medicine. You may already be familiar with or even have experienced energy techniques that manipulate chi, such as; acupuncture, acupressure, Reiki and Shiatsu, which are also founded from these same Eastern roots. The field of study around our chi energy system is vast and complex so my aim here is to provide you with an appreciation of some simple concepts that you can relate to in order to understand some of these energetic influences in your game. In becoming more aware you may find it easier to be kind on yourself and you will have more tools with which to raise your awareness to the triggers that cause you to underperform. Further reading is always recommended for those more interested in finding out more detail on this topic.

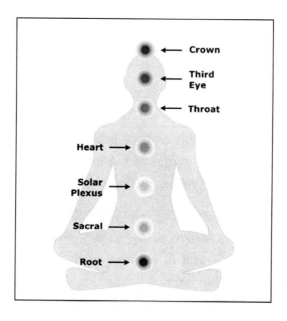

Fig 4. Main Chakra Locations

The chakras diagram at Fig 4. above shows where each main chakra is located on your body. The 7 chakras run from the first chakra at the base of your body, up your body to the 7th chakra at the top of your head; your crown. We will explore each of the 7 main chakras in turn so that you can appreciate how they link with specific attributes in your tennis. This is very important because when we have a clear flow of energy throughout our system we can achieve a balanced mental, emotional and physical life. As a result of this balance we are able to achieve our potential in whatever we are doing. Imbalances in our energy system can be caused by a wide range of factors, from chemicals that we put into our system whether in the form of food additives, toxins such as alcohol or drugs, prescription drugs or external toxins such as car emissions etc.

Whilst there are some of these external sources that we can control, such as alcohol, drugs, diet and the like there are also external sources that we may not be able to control. You need to focus on changing that which is within your control rather than putting your energy into things that you cannot control.

Factors that you can control, that are considered to strongly influence your energy system, are the thoughts and feelings you experience, how you handle traumatic situations, what you believe about yourself and what you think others believe about you. Your thoughts and feelings are psychological factors that not only influence your energetic performance but they can also have an impact on things such as injuries and your recovery from injuries, your general health and wellbeing, stamina and other aspects of your physical functioning.

Your energy system and how it is functioning is therefore a major contributor to your development and your ability to play your best more often. So let's look at 7 of the major energy centres in your body and their impact on your performance, both positive and negative.

Your "chi" is you life force and has a significant impact on your performance physically, mentally, emotionally and physiologically. This energy flows in and out of your body through your chakras and runs within your body through your meridians. Blockages or imbalances in this energy system can cause you to underperform. When your energy system is balanced you can achieve your peak performance. Your thoughts and feelings influence your energetic performance in tennis and can also impact things such as injuries, recovery from injuries, general health, wellbeing and stamina, etc.

BASE OR ROOT CHAKRA

The first chakra, known as the base or root chakra is at the base of your body, between your legs, and it is linked to your sense of tribal and group interactions. It is associated with the colour red and aligned with the following:

- loyalty, commitment and support within the group
- sense of physical identity
- survival instincts, security, physical health and fitness
- sense of prejudice and belonging
- sense of direction

The first chakra then, is responsible for our level of commitment to the "group". Where loyalty to the group or team is an important attribute, i.e. in team sports, the base chakra energy comes into its own. However, when the first chakra is out of balance, either over or under functioning, this strength of loyalty can be followed to the detriment of one's own personal needs and desires.

The player who has an imbalance in their first chakra may struggle with their own sense of direction or even feel a sense of lack of belonging. An attitude of "warfare" may be dominant, or prejudice so a tennis player may feel threatened at a physical level if they lose or are the weakest in a team event. Because this chakra is also about physical survival and security, players with an imbalance in this energy centre may struggle to feel secure in their game and so their confidence can easily suffer.

Players strongly driven at this level of energy will only change their performance at the pace of the group to which they are attached. So, where a player has a strong commitment to their own family and coaching team, if the family and team are averse to change, the player will be and feel inhibited from changing, no matter how much they might personally want to change.

For a player to become the best that they can, they will need to be able to deal with moving away from this group energy. When I say moving away I am not referring to physically moving away from your family and coaching team, although sometimes that can be necessary at some point. I am referring to the fact that the player needs to learn to stand up for themselves within the group, which may mean they no longer support the group ideals. It means standing alone and standing up for what you want; you will need to learn to put yourself first and take responsibility for achieving your dreams. Some great players have done this by moving away from strong parental and/or coaching influences at some point in their career.

> Believe anything that supports you and do what is right for you. Others may disagree and that is their problem.

SACRAL CHAKRA

The second chakra is known as the sacral chakra and is located about 2 inches below your navel. It is directly linked to the giving and receiving of pleasure and our one-to-one relationships. It is associated with the colour orange and aligned with the following:

- ➢ emotions

- ➢ sexuality and sexual expression

- ➢ feelings, desires, sensations and movement

- ➢ your ability to accept change

- ➢ social awareness and isolation

Players with an imbalance in their second chakra energy may struggle when it comes to being competitive, either being over competitive or not at all competitive. The feeling of a loss of power in relation to other players, feeling powerless and unable to compete can also be a function of an imbalance in this energy.

If a player struggles to get any pleasure out of the game, it is a possible indication that there is a block in the second chakra. Lower back and hip problems are also indicators of an imbalance in this chakra's energy and often closely related to insecurity and instability.

Since this chakra is also linked to one-to-one relationships, an imbalance in the energy flow through this chakra will also be experienced in a player's sexual relationships. Although what a player does off court is not the concern of this book, an imbalance in this chakra, as with all chakras, will influence your tennis performance. You can see this when you look at the number of players whose performance has changed one way or another as function of changes in their personal relationships.

> Take pleasure out of everything that you do and accept the uncertainties that are always a part of the game.

SOLAR PLEXUS

The third chakra is known as our solar plexus and is located about 2 inches above our navel. It is directly linked to our sense of self. It is associated with the colour yellow and is aligned with the following:

- ➤ ego identity
- ➤ freedom
- ➤ personal will and power

> ➢ spontaneity and non-dominating power

> ➢ generosity and morality

> ➢ self-confidence and courage

> ➢ ambition

> ➢ anger

> ➢ satisfaction and contentment

The third chakra is your personal power house. It is linked to your sense of identity and self-confidence. Low self-confidence is probably one of the biggest causes of poor performance for many players. Players who are unable to control their emotions and specifically anger are likely to be suffering an imbalance in this energy centre; basically, their confidence and identity are not yet well developed.

A lack of personal ambition and drive could also be indicators of an imbalance in your third chakra. When this chakra is functioning well you will see the strength of character that we might consider "charismatic", someone who is generous towards others without martyring themselves, has an openness, self-honesty and humbleness that we would more likely associate with a spiritual leader than a tennis player. Confident, unassuming and powerful would be the attributes of the positive functioning of this chakra.

Be strong and courageous even if you don't feel like it.

HEART CHAKRA

The fourth chakra bridges the gap between the 3 lower chakras and the 3 higher chakras in our body. In other words it bridges the gap between our physical reality and our conceptual self. It is known as the heart chakra and is located in the area of the heart. It is linked with the colours green and pink and is aligned with the following:

> love (of self and others)

> integration of opposites such as mind & body, male & female

> compassion

> sense of centeredness and peace

> sense of true nature and purity

As they say, "if your heart isn't in it, it isn't happening!" Players who have their heart chakra functioning well will be performing for the sheer joy and pleasure of the experience. They will not need to prove themselves, nor will they be competing against the other player (the need to prove oneself is an energy that comes from the first 3 chakras). They will be competing for themselves and against themselves, for their own personal sense of achievement.

They will be balanced in their analysis of the game and give compassion to themselves in defeat and failure. They will have a sense of passion for the game that is based around their love of the game rather than being driven by their second chakra sense of competitive power against their opponent. They are also more likely to perform through balance, from both their heart and head. An imbalance in this area can result in players operating too much out of their head, being too critical, analytical, logical and rational.

> Be compassionate in defeat and humble in your successes.

THROAT CHAKRA

The fifth chakra is known as your throat chakra and is located in your throat area. It is linked to your will to carry out ideas that come through your sixth chakra. It is linked to the colour indigo blue and aligned with:

- ➢ your creative identity, dreaming & self expression
- ➢ active listening & communication
- ➢ language, diplomacy, remorse
- ➢ sense of superiority
- ➢ the power of choice

The fifth chakra is about your expression of your self; your will to carry out your desires and ideas. Your ideas come from your sixth chakra. It is also related to your power of choice and communication.

Players who are stuck in the energies of the lower 3 chakras may struggle to realise their dreams, since their dreams need the energy of this chakra to be supporting them. If a player is struggling to achieve their peak potential it will be essentially through fear and a lack of awareness. For example, if you are strongly tied in energetically to the tribal energy system of the base chakra you may not be aware that you have the power of choice. You will effectively compromise your own dreams because you feel you don't have the power to do anything about it. Your confidence will be so badly affected that no matter what you decide you really want to do, you just don't believe you will be able to make it happen.

Throat, neck and shoulder problems, thyroid, voice, ears, lungs, arms and hands are all areas of the body that can be affected by an imbalance in the energy of this area. Your desire to express yourself through playing tennis is a function of the fifth chakra's energy. If you are not achieving the results you want, you are effectively holding yourself back with your self expression, which will potentially hurt you in the future.

Express yourself, be creative and speak your truth.

THIRD EYE CHAKRA

The sixth chakra is known as your third eye chakra and is located between your eyes. It is linked to your ability to assimilate ideas and concepts. It is linked to the colour violet blue and is aligned with the following:

> ➢ your higher intuition

> ➢ psychic ability

> ➢ your ability to carry out your ideas

> ➢ clarity, forgiveness compassion

> ➢ the centre of your true motivation

The sixth chakra consciously directs your activities and is the place your ideas are realised. Your image of being No. 1 in the world is first experienced here, in your head. So this is the chakra that influences your ability to create your inner vision and to carry out those ideas. Players not being true to their inner vision are likely to experience an imbalance in this area. Stress experienced through migraines, headaches, neck tension, eye problems and learning difficulties are considered to be influenced by the energy in this chakra.

For a player to become the best that they can be, they need to be able to go through with their plan, to go out and act on their dreams and desires. A player's sense of intuition is also a function of this chakra and in this sense I am particularly referring to the intuitive sense that you are doing what is right for you. That sense of knowing you are on the right track. It is not a gut instinct; it is a sense of knowing. The sixth chakra is the controller of this energy.

Follow your dreams, knowing that you cannot
know how it will work out.

CROWN CHAKRA

The seventh chakra is known as the crown chakra and is located on the top of your head. It is our link with the universal life force energy. Its colour is violet and it is aligned with the following:

> ➢ universal identity

> ➢ thought processes, self knowledge, awareness

> ➢ spiritual connection, wisdom, enlightenment and joy

> ➢ understanding and empathy

> ➢ perception of reality and self

> ➢ relationship with authority

> ➢ sense of direction and life purpose

The seventh chakra energy is responsible for a higher level of functioning, linking us to the universe; the all is one concept. However, within tennis this chakra's energy revolves around the player's realisation of the role that tennis plays in their life. Players with a balanced functioning will be more likely to see tennis as a game and a contribution to their experiences in life rather than seeing tennis as a reflection of them as a person. They will have a strong and accurate perception of their performance since they will no longer be in denial, fear or feeling inadequate. They will recognise their contribution as part of the overall plan for their journey in this life and begin to see the wider impact of their success, both in the context of their overall development and in the future of tennis.

Remind yourself that there is more to life than tennis
and of how much tennis contributes to your life
and development as a person.

Rebalancing and unblocking your energy system as part of your personal training is recommended and can be done using professional energy techniques such as Reiki, Shiatsu, Acupuncture and other variations of these. Following the specific guidance in the grey boxes will also help you to maintain a healthy balance.

Meditation is another great way to learn to balance your energy. I will talk more about how to do this in Section 3.

8

Attracting the Results That You Want

The *Law of Attraction* is a concept that is becoming more familiar with recent releases of films and books, such as "What the Bleep" and "The Secret". Many players though are still not yet aware of the power of their thoughts, beliefs and language in creating the results that they get.

Your language is a powerful driver in creating your results. If at first that seems a scary concept and you're worried about having to think about everything you say, stop and learn how it really works.

One of the first rules in attracting what you want is that "like attracts like". That which is like unto itself is drawn. When it comes to the Law of Attraction it is not the case that opposites attract at all. Energetically, something will attract anything else that holds the same vibrational frequency as itself. You will know this yourself as you tend to like people you have things in common with. It is easier for you to feel connected to people who think like you do. Your social groups will be a good example of this. One of the things that can hinder your achievement of peak potential is linked to this notion of like attracting like. When you change and develop yourself, your friends may no longer be operating at the same energetic frequency that matches yours. You will find you have less in common and begin to feel more detached from them. When players make major changes in their performance, sometimes their social networks are affected. This can be very difficult for some players to handle, to the extent that they can hold back their progress for the sake of maintaining their friendships.

Also, remind yourself of the fact that at an unconscious level we do not process negative language or the absence of something. So, if you say to yourself "don't hit the ball in the net" you will automatically create in your mind the image of hitting the ball into the net. Although you can understand what that message means at the conscious thinking level because you can take steps in your mind to process the words you are saying, you are actually giving your energy to the idea of hitting the ball in the net, since that is the image that you have created. Now, because you created the image of hitting the ball in the net you are more likely to attract that as a result.

The universe doesn't process negatives either, so whatever you give your attention to, whether you want it or not, you will be more likely to attract that thing. So if you really don't want to lose and you keep saying to yourself "don't lose", then you are likely to attract exactly what you don't want – losing. Which means that, no matter how you are playing in the game, you must give your attention to what you want to achieve rather than what you are doing wrong or what might go wrong in the future.

So what enables us to attract more or less of what we want? Your emotions! The stronger your emotion towards something the more likely it is to manifest. So if you feel strongly about not wanting to lose then you will be more likely to attract "losing" than a player who doesn't care too much about whether they lose or not. And remember a really strong desire to win can often be a really strong desire not to lose in disguise!

Always remember, a strong emotion will boost the manifestation of what your attention is focused on, even if that is something you don't really want.

So how do you go about attracting more of what you want to achieve in your game and less of what you don't want? Firstly, you need to become more aware of the language that you use on a regular basis. Your language is constantly brainwashing you. Every time you think a thought or say something to yourself you are brainwashing yourself and you cannot stop it. Ask yourself, if your coach was saying to you what you say or think to yourself, would you feel empowered, confident and successful? I bet, if your coach spoke to you the way you speak to yourself, you would very quickly want to sack them! You must raise your awareness to change your language and to start brainwashing yourself with empowering thoughts.

To identify the things you are saying to yourself, (which in the heat of the moment you may feel are absolutely deserving and true) you will need to overcome your desire for the truth and replace it with a desire for compassion towards yourself. You must begin this process of self-awareness with kindness towards yourself otherwise you will become both confused and frustrated, which defeats the objective.

If you know you are a player who consistently berates yourself on court then you need to commit to changing what you say to yourself and what you say about your play...and here's the thing, you need to make those changes to what you say to yourself irrespective of your results. There are plenty of challenges in the game that are more worthy of your attention than constantly beating yourself up for being human!

Remember that like attracts like so if you think positively you are more likely to attract what you want. The universe and your mind does not process things that are phrased in negative language, so focus on what you want rather than what you don't. Drop the word's not, can't, and don't from your language. The more emotion the greater the chance of you manifesting what you are focusing on, so strong negative emotions will be likely to create for you more of the thing that caused the emotion in the first place. Watch your language and work hard to brainwash yourself with things you want to believe and hear and be compassionate with yourself when you think you are failing. You are doing your best.

THE POWER OF INTENTION

Let's look in a bit more detail at how the Law of Attraction works and what you need to do to create the results you want more often.

Firstly, you must set out your intention. In other words you must set out what you want to achieve. There are several ways that a player can do this which will result in them attracting a less than desired result. For example, if your intention, or let's call it desire, is to win the tournament, you will say to yourself "I really want to win this tournament". But, for the Law of Attraction to work, that intention has to be "clean". In other words if you say to yourself that you really want to win this tournament and then deep down inside you get a "...but", or "...if" tagging along before or after your intention, then your intention is not clean.

An example of a "but" and "if", would be, "I really want to win this tournament, "but" clay is not my favourite surface". "I can win this tournament "if" I get a good draw". Both of these are statements that a player may think or say to themselves, or even say to others. They are unclean because they are conditional and therefore the intention will be weakened. In other words the intention is not driven by belief and desire. Conditional intentions are weaker in their ability to manifest the result than a pure intention to win would be.

Many players will also throw into this mix here the notion of whether it is "realistic" for them to be able to win, because they will have done some calculation in their mind about the probabilities of beating someone seeded or rated better than them. These probability calculations are a block to attracting the result you want. Just ask yourself, has anyone else ever beaten players who are better than them? The answer of course is yes, so if the answer is yes the only thing stopping you doing the same is...you! The more open you can be in your thinking the more opportunities you will give yourself.

Use clean language when you think about what you want – no "ifs" and no "buts" and avoid making any judgments of probability of your chances in the game.

BELIEF

The second step is that you believe you can have what you want; that you deserve it and can achieve it. Again, as a player you will have mental thinking patterns, learned behaviours and attitudes that prevent you having total belief in your ability to win the match or tournament. Of course, from your analytical, logical, rational, left brain functioning, your calculations can be perfectly reasonable and may even be true. And you can be assured that they will manifest as true if you believe them! A player's belief in their ability may have certain conditions that apply; i.e. "I can believe in myself if my service is on form", or "I can believe in myself if I get a good start in the game".

To achieve your highest potential you need to believe in yourself with a mental/emotional and spiritual strength that takes you well beyond your errors. Great players continue to believe in themselves until after the last point has been played. Lesser players stop believing well before that time and may even start a tournament without believing in themselves.

So one of the difficulties for any player, (which is what stops many players taking full advantage of the Law of Attraction) is continuing to believe in yourself even when you aren't getting the results you want. We currently live in a quick fix, results now, fast food, fast everything society. Players expect their success to come quickly and when it doesn't come as quickly as they would like they lose faith. The problem is that they are losing faith in themselves, which can only lead to problems further down the line. Persistence is a key skill that is linked to developing your self belief. No player ever became successful without being persistent in the pursuit of their goal.

Players must recognise that they have to keep believing in themselves even when they are not getting the results they want, and they also need to be working on all aspects of their game so that they know they have a good reason to believe. In other words, if as a player I believe in myself and yet I am not working on my game, then not a lot is going to happen. I can believe in myself all I want, but I am unlikely to make anything happen by sitting on my proverbial backside.

> Believe only those things that help your game and don't believe things that limit you. If something puts a boundary in place, it is stopping you in some way, then don't believe it! Believe irrespective of how well you are doing in any one specific moment.

ACTION

So the third step in making the Law of Attraction work for you is to continue to take action to get what you want no matter what results you are getting. That means becoming aware of what you are currently doing that is contributing to your results (mental/energetic, physical, technical, tactical) and make the changes that you need to make to progress your game.

Most players in this current climate will look at the categories I have listed of mental/energetic, physical, technical and tactical and I can pretty much guarantee will firstly address technical then perhaps tactical then physical and most often last on the list, if at all, will be mental/energetic. Yet the mental and energetic aspects underpin a great deal of development in the other 3 areas.

The place to look to make the changes could be the place you feel most uncomfortable about addressing. The area that causes you the most discomfort is likely to be something that you fear. If you have a fear around changing something, you will not change it and it will hold you back. So, it's time to be brave and face your fears so that you can fully utilise the Law of Attraction and get the results you want.

Just do it. Get out there and go for what you want and promise yourself that you will do whatever it takes to get what you want.

9

Why Positive Thinking is Scary

Why is positive thinking such a scary thing for most players? Of course there will be some players who will say that positive thinking isn't scary and yet they still don't do it! Whether you think it is or isn't scary, positive thinking is something that as a player you may do for a short period of time, but very quickly you will go back to old habits. And that means giving your attention to what you did that wasn't right, what might go wrong later and/or beating yourself up for making mistakes. Some players would love to think positively but daren't. Why?

One of the problems that can arise when a player is told to think positively is that it can lead them to raise their expectations of their performance. Many players will have got into the habit of putting themselves down, under stating their chances or being coy about how well they are playing, especially in front of their peers. Often this is a way of protecting their feelings if they don't do as well as they feel they should.

Positive thinking can encourage the process of raising one's expectations. This becomes a problem when those expectations are not achieved, the result is feeling you have let yourself down and therefore positive thinking doesn't work. It seems that we often prefer to have low expectations for ourselves so that we can exceed them and feel good. Setting low expectations is a poor strategy since you are constantly undervaluing your performance, undermining your abilities and subsequently damaging your self-esteem and confidence.

Positive thinking can easily take players out of their comfort zones again, in part, because of the expectation that if you are talking positively to yourself you should play better. Players then struggle with positive thinking when they are not playing well because they don't feel they deserve to be kind to themselves.

Positive thinking requires you to put yourself out there, to do what others aren't overtly doing; to be kind to yourself, even when your results may not justify it according to your conscious analytical critical mind.

Players can falsely believe that if they talk positively they should play better. Sadly, if only it were that easy! Thinking positively and saying positive things to yourself doesn't guarantee your results. Just because you say all the right things doesn't mean it will happen that way. But certainly by not saying the right things you are setting yourself up for failure more often than not. Positive thinking stimulates different neurological pathways from negative thinking and has a higher energy frequency, which means when you think positively you will feel better about yourself and your game, even when your results are not as perfect as you would like.

Positive thinking has to be done with the belief that if you continue thinking positively, overall, you will get better results and achieve your best performances more often. Players who think negatively and undermine themselves will limit their ability and never perform as well as they could have done with more positive thinking. But, hey, they will of course be right!

To change this in yourself you simply need to have the desire to improve, the discipline to take action by changing your thinking and the will to be gentle and supportive with yourself when you aren't doing as well as you would like.

Positive thinking is a habit and something you need to do consistently and that may mean being positive when you don't quite feel that way. Be persistent in your positivity and make sure that you keep your expectations in check. Just because you think positively doesn't guarantee you will play well, but it certainly helps you more than thinking negatively – unless you just want to be right!

10

Being True To YOU

I am sure that you are coming to realise, if you hadn't already, what a wonderfully exquisite and complex system the human mind and body is. We are receiving energetic signals and messages throughout our body all the time. I am sure every player has experienced that sensation we call "gut instincts", perhaps about a game or an opponent or the venue, or aspects of their training. Being true to yourself as a player is about following what is right for you. Whether you recognise what it means to be true to yourself is not important at this stage. What is important is that you are aware of the impact that being true to yourself has on your game.

When you are true to yourself you are essentially building your self-esteem. Self-esteem is a significant ingredient in the development of success and self-fulfilment in all areas of your life. With low self-esteem you will be unable to achieve your highest potential, your performances will be inconsistent, and where you align your performance outcomes to your self-esteem, you can easily suffer with behavioural problems such as depression, anxiety, withdrawal from social interactions and even quitting the game.

Self-esteem is fundamental to you achieving personal power in your life and essential for you as a player who strives to achieve great success in the game. The key to achieving high self-esteem is being true to yourself. To know what it means to be true to yourself you need to get in touch with your gut instincts and feelings and learn to interpret them, rather than hide and run away from them. So, let's explore how you can do that. Below are some examples that you might have experienced where you will have NOT been true to yourself.

1. You really wanted to do something but did not do it because someone wanted you to do something else

2. You have not really wanted to play in an event but gone ahead anyway

3. You have wanted to do something but not done it because to do so might upset someone

4. You didn't want your parents watching you but you couldn't tell them

5. Your coach wants you to change some aspect of your game but you don't tell them of your concerns about changing it and go ahead anyway

6. You want some quiet time before a match starts but your friends want you to chat with them so you do what they want

7. You want to get to the venue early but someone asks you to do them a favour so you do and get to the venue later than you wanted

8. You wanted your coach or parents to be there but didn't push for that to happen

9. You want a particular racket, but someone talks you into something else that you don't quite feel is right for you

The list of events in which as a player you can undermine your self-esteem by not being true to yourself is endless. When you are not being true to yourself you are in fact compromising yourself. Although these things may seem like small events, the impact can be significant in your performance. Take number 7 above, "wanting to turn up early for the match and doing someone else a favour so you turn up later than you wanted". How do you then feel when you start the match poorly because you don't feel fully warmed up? How do you feel when you subsequently lose that match? You may want to blame the person who stopped you getting to the game early, but the reality is that the fault lies with you. And deep down inside you will know it. You have not given yourself the best opportunity to perform and you have let yourself down. Unfortunately, you only have yourself to blame and you may also feel bad about the fact that you didn't do as you wanted. In that situation, it can be easy to begin to resent those who called on your time, when actually it is still down to you. You did not go with what you truly wanted to do.

Speaking your truth, saying how it is for you and being honest with those you are working with are all critical to your development as a player and the achievement of your peak potential. Many players struggle with speaking their truth for fear of upsetting others. Younger players can particularly struggle as they are often brought up to do as they are told rather than express their true desires. And of course, a player who learns to speak their truth must also be able to take the feedback that comes from their coach/parents in such interactions, which can be tough. All parties need to be able to sensibly debate and relate; all parties need to be able to speak their truth. Remember every person has a different way of interpreting their experience, we all have a different model of the world and therefore being true to yourself is your right as a person.

During training, performances, preparation and all other activities related to your game, you will experience a sensation of "yes that feels right to me" or "no that doesn't feel right to me". These feelings may happen in respect of decisions you are taking about your training programme, or maybe in the context of selecting particular tournaments to enter, or who you want on your team. Most often you become aware of how you are feeling about something because you get a sensation in your gut; your solar plexus area, about 2 inches above your navel.

You will experience feelings during the game and during your training, when things are going well and when they are not. The difficulty is how to interpret these sensations, are they good or bad? What are they trying to tell you? One simple way to tell what the feeling is about is to identify what you were thinking of at the time, or just before, the feeling. An easy feeling to come to understand is fear or that lesser form of fear known as nerves or anxiety. There are likely to be specific times in a match such as the first serve of the game, big points, closing out games, match points, etc that elicit in you a rise in nervousness or anxiety. The extent of the anxiety feeling will always be influenced by what you are thinking, or more deeply, by your beliefs about the situation.

For example, if you are thinking, "I must get this in" the level of nerves that you experience is likely (for most of you) to be higher than if you think to yourself, "Great I love these points". "I must get this in" is like saying to yourself, "I must get this in... or something bad will happen". No-one likes anything bad happening to them and when you think something bad is going to happen you set off your natural fight or flight response, which can be experienced as an increase in the nervous feeling. On the other hand, when you say to yourself "Great I love these points, this is so much fun" there is no threat attached to it. Therefore your physiological response will be a healthy one; some anxiety, which is necessary for a great performance and a focus on what you need to do.

An example of this process where your beliefs are concerned would be in the case of holding a belief that you always lose to a certain player. If you hold that belief and find yourself serving for the game you will experience more anxiety serving out the match than you would do if you held a more healthy belief, like "I believe I am playing great and can beat this player today". So, rather than interpret your feelings as simply good or bad, look for what you are saying to yourself or your beliefs that are linked to the feeling. Good feelings are better for your performance than negative feelings. Anxiety at an appropriate level, such as that butterfly feeling you get at key moments is a good indicator that your body is ready to perform. Please begin to see this level of anxiety as something positive rather than negative. Embrace it. Excessive anxiety and tension are indicators that you are thinking something that is detrimental to your performance. Becoming more aware of the thoughts that you have when you experience emotions, will give you a clear indicator as to what you need to change.

Being true to yourself is to always align your actions with your desires. In this way you can experience a healthy feeling. You are likely to feel nerves or anxiety if you are pushing yourself outside of your comfort zone, but you need to do this to achieve peak performance. Not being true to yourself is to run away from your feelings without understanding what they are saying to you. Not being true to yourself is to not do what you really feel is right for you because of the influence of others. It is also not doing what you want to avoid the negative consequences that you perceive will happen. When you are being true to yourself, your personal power becomes stronger and your sense of self-esteem increases. You feel good about yourself because you are acting on your desires.

Being true to yourself is about speaking your truth and not allowing others to distract you. It is about giving to yourself. When you are true to yourself, your sense of self-esteem and confidence will be higher, you will feel in control of your game and your life. You will recognise your qualities and you will be taking responsibility for your game. Learn to use your feelings to develop your performance rather than running away from them. You can do this by noticing the underlying thinking patterns. You were born to be the best that you can be. Don't let fear stop you.

11

The Problem
With Emotions

Your emotions have a huge impact on your life. They provide depth to your experience. Without them, your life would be empty. Simply, they impact: your ability to think, your physical arousal and your energetic balance. All in all, they can really mess up your performance, whether the emotions are good or bad!

I have often watched young players and especially boys, in the throws of their game, toughing it out like two young peacocks, each trying to assert themselves on the other player. During this display, one young peacock will thrust his fist in the face of the other as a triumphant gesture as if daring his opponent to rise to the challenge or concede. This act of defiance towards the opponent and the fist pumped gesticulation of triumph over another can easily have a detrimental affect on the player himself rather than his opponent, because the intention behind the fist pumping is misplaced.

Tennis in essence requires significant use of the fine muscles in your body, requiring a deft touch, skill, grace, balance and execution to the finest degrees of accuracy. Power comes from appropriate use of your muscles. In this sense tennis is best played at slightly lower levels of adrenalin, also known as levels of arousal, than some other sports such as rugby and football. The level of adrenalin that is surging around your body will influence your state of "readiness" and your ability to perform at your highest level. With lower levels of adrenalin you may experience lethargy, tiredness, sleepiness, apathy and lack of energy. With higher levels of adrenalin you can experience negative emotions such as anger, frustration, stress, panic, fear, and over excitement. At either extreme of adrenalin, low or high, performance is negatively affected. Therefore the optimum adrenalin functioning is somewhere in the middle and for most tennis players it will be short of the midline, slightly lower rather than slightly higher.

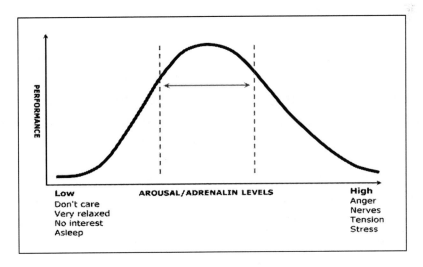

Fig 5. Arousal & Adrenalin Curve

In Fig 5. above, we can see the way adrenalin affects performance. The thick black line indicates the flow of adrenalin, starting low, building to a peak and then dropping off. Please be aware that although the level of adrenaline in your system will drop off relatively slowly, the deterioration in your performance can be very rapid, like a crash or explosion.

Through knowledge and experience, professionals are often better able to control their levels of adrenalin. Even when they blow up out of frustration, their expression of that emotion can be short lived and they get their full attention back to the game more quickly than most amateurs.

Other players and juniors in particular are unlikely to be aware of the impact of their jubilant fist thrusting and less than jubilant temper tantrums. They do not control their explosions and do not recover and get back into the game. What we usually see is the build up of emotion, during which progressively more mistakes are made. Then one mistake breaks the proverbial camels back, which results in the player displaying negative emotion. This can be easily followed by another period of less than effective play, followed by another explosion of emotion and so it goes on. At some point later in the game, often when all hope of winning has gone, or when the adrenalin levels have returned to a more optimum level because of the player "giving up" you may see a period of being back in the game again.

The length of time it takes a player to refocus on the game will depend on factors such as the intensity of the emotion and how frequently they re-run the movie of their failures over in their mind. The player can maintain the impact of the negative emotion for a number of points or even games, to the overall detriment of their performance. In many instances it is the emotion that has destroyed the player's game and not a technical error. But, instead of managing their emotion they have been too busy, either stuck in their emotional outburst and just hitting the ball harder hoping it will go in, or trying to resolve the technical error that they think caused the mistakes.

Tennis is best played at lower levels of adrenalin so as to enable fine muscle movements in the execution of shots. Controlling the level of adrenalin you experience can be done by controlling your emotions. Negative emotions can easily lead to a quick deterioration in performance.

EMOTIONAL CONTROL

A very simple way to reduce excessive adrenalin is to engage in deep belly breathing. The key to deep belly breathing for a player who is experiencing strong feelings is that they must focus their attention on their breathing. Doing deep belly breathing without giving your total attention to it will have little effect. This requires practice since belly breathing in the heat of the moment is not easy to do.

Belly breathing is more easily learned lying down as that is a more relaxed position. The objective is to breathe deep into your belly, through your nose, in and out, as if you are blowing up a balloon in your stomach, below your rib cage. You are filling the lower part of your lungs but it feels like it is going into your belly. It should not be forced breathing but instead relaxed breathing that gently expands the stomach area. When doing this breathing your shoulders should remain quite still, they should not be rising and falling.

Doing belly breathing every night whilst lying in bed is a great and easy way to practice, but you also need to integrate it into your training, when you get uptight and then of course into your competitive performance.

If as a player you are low on adrenalin, feeling lethargic, then the best way to get adrenalin up is to run around a bit and start thinking about things that excite you and make you feel good. A key to achieving success here is to say to yourself that you are feeling energised and ready to go, even if at first you don't feel that way. If you are running around telling yourself you feel tired, guess what... you will feel tired. So, what you say to yourself will influence the level of adrenalin you experience in your body.

Overall, if you are a player who experiences strong emotions during the game, as a general principle emotions are better being released than stored. Ideally, in releasing your emotions you should avoid any form of equipment or personal abuse and release the emotions as you go through the game rather than wait until they build to a crescendo. One way to release emotion as you go through the game is to make sure you breathe out as you hit the ball, this can be done with a grunt too for those that need further assistance. The grunt should sound rhythmical and balanced rather than changing in its tone and pitch. Some players find grunting unacceptable, but as a release of negative emotion it can work really well, so you must decide for yourself whether to use it or not. You should also practice bringing your attention back to the point you are about to play once you have released the energy. With your focus on what you want to achieve your energy will then be directed on what you want rather than the error that caused you to feel the emotion.

However, learning to not experience negative emotions is an even more powerful way to get the best out of your performance. Negative emotions are destructive to your game every time. In no instance does negative emotion help your game because it is a stressor to your body. It is a negative form of energy and will always result in you underperforming. Remember that slight nerves are okay for your performance providing you are feeling them as an excitement rather than a worry. To do this you just need to say to yourself that you love these butterfly feelings as they mean you are ready to go.

Excessive adrenalin can be reduced through deep belly breathing and this should be included as part of your between point routines to stop the build up of adrenalin. Low adrenalin is less likely to be an issue and can be helped through exercise and getting focused. Learning to not experience emotions (not simply holding them in) is a powerful way to stay in control.

12

Channelling Anger

Anger and frustration are two of the most common emotions that players experience and yet they are highly destructive when not channelled into generating a stronger performance. For the player that turns anger in on themselves their play will deteriorate rapidly and in the longer term there is a significant chance of health problems too.

Before deciding whether anger is a problem for you, it is important to recognise that anger manifests in many different ways. The most obvious that we think of is the externalised anger seen as the racket gets smashed against the floor or back netting or as balls are sent into orbit. Overt displays of anger are only one expression of anger and we tend to see this more with boys than girls. However, internalised anger is equally as destructive. It is thought that internalised anger can manifest as depression and I believe this to be true. Anger is also strongly linked with heart disease and blood pressure problems.

As a general principle, anger is better off expressed than internalised and if you can learn to live without it, then so much the better. The first step to living without anger is recognising that you choose your emotions, something you are aware of from the first section of this book. Your emotions are a function of your internal representation. That internal representation is a function of how you filter your external experiences. Anger can often be a symptom of control issues, with players getting angry about things that are not within their control. Feeling that you should be able to achieve something and then don't can lead to anger because you think you should be able to control the outcome. To help you control anger only give your attention to those things you can control and let go of things you cannot control. You are unlikely to think straight if you allow anger to get to you. You cannot control the results; you can control your own game, your emotional state, your thinking, your tactics, your interpretation of the game, and your feelings about yourself. You can only influence what your opponent does by how you control your own performance.

Mike Fisher's (2005) book, *"Beating Anger"*, gives a detailed account of how to recognise the different aspects of anger and how to deal with it. It is a book I highly recommend to players who have problems in this area. Sadly, for many players who experience strong explosions of anger, with associated behaviours such as racket breaking, what often follows is remorse and guilt. Anger is a recipe for disaster.

Players who struggle with anger can find great reasons to continue with it as they will on the odd occasion hit a fantastic winner that they attribute to the fact that they were really irritated and angry. What they fail to realise is that it is not the anger that caused them to hit the winner. In fact, what they have done is used their anger to direct their focus in a very strong and powerful way. So, many players miss the point and think the anger works for them. This is more often the case with younger players. I have also had players quote the great John McEnroe as an example of the fact that anger can help your performance. Firstly, even if John McEnroe's performance was in fact enhanced by his anger, which we cannot know for sure because we cannot know how good he could have been without his outbursts, he is one of very few players who could carry this off and he will have done so because he channelled his anger to focus his attention.

Secondly, I don't actually believe that John's outbursts were as angry as they appeared and were more likely to have been used as a way of letting go of the point and redirecting his focus into the game. To express yourself when you feel you have been wronged, as with a line call, can help let go of the frustration. John, for the most part, channelled his frustration into performing better. Eventually, of course his outbursts became part of the performance; he became identified with them. His outbursts created more of a distraction and his opponents were more likely to be put off than him by his displays. John was too smart a player to allow his game to be destroyed by an emotion!

Now, let's be straight here. Anger is simply a feeling, and since it is a feeling it will be experienced as a function of the thinking patterns or beliefs that precede it. Players generally become angry when they are not doing as well as they expected, not getting the result they want and/or they are not controlling the game as they feel they should.

Cheating behaviours, opponents who get lucky, net cord wins and any other unfairness will be a challenge to a player and may result in them experiencing anger. In essence, when things aren't going their way they blow up! Players get angry because they can't control what is happening, they are angry with themselves for not being in control and for making mistakes that they shouldn't.

However, it is only this way because of the beliefs or rules the player is running in their mind about what is fair and what should be happening. If they didn't hold those rules, beliefs and expectations in place they wouldn't experience anger. Otherwise all players would experience anger and they don't. How the player is processing their experience will influence how they respond. For example, if you hold a belief or a rule in your mind that you should make all easy balls count and you don't do that, when you then hit an easy ball out of the court you will see that as a significant error rather than seeing all the great work you had done to get to that stage. Because you are seeing the result as something that breaks your rules you will feel bad about it in some way. Whereas a player who doesn't hold the rule that they should make all easy balls, but instead is running a rule that says, create as many opportunities in the game as you can, will respond differently to the same result, because they will look at the fact that they created a great opportunity.

In this sense you must remember that you are choosing anger as an internal response to what is happening outside of you! You are choosing to respond to the situation with anger rather than put your energy into achieving the results you want. Channelling anger is about redirecting the energy that you experience through anger into the game. To do this effectively requires that you focus on what you want rather than what is happening to cause the anger in the first place.

Channelling the emotion of anger, is channelling your focus and intention, and I would add, that it is best to channel your focus and intention into your performance objectives; serving solidly, running every ball down, pushing the player deep and wide, playing good margins etc. rather than into "winning" which you have little control over.

Players who are results focused rather than performance focused are more likely to become angry simply because they don't have full control of the outcome. Players who focus on performance objectives rather than outcomes/results feel more in control, because they are focusing on what they can control rather than what they cannot.

One technique that can really help if you are feeling angry is to stand still and breathe deeply. Standing still is a key factor in this technique because it is helping you to become grounded. As you stand still you need to imagine the energy of anger travelling down through your body, down your legs and out of your feet into the ground. Most players when they feel angry want to move around a lot, a fidgety kind of movement, but this exacerbates the anger. Stand still and breathe deeply into your lower belly for as long as possible. Now I realise this can be tricky in the middle of an active sport like tennis, but there are times when this is possible. You can stand still and visualise any frustration moving down your body and out through your feet even before it builds up into full blown anger, during the time between games. Essentially, though you need to also be working on challenging the rules you are running that cause you to feel angry.

Anger is highly destructive to performance and your health. You must learn to focus on what you can control. Learning to work with performance objectives rather than just outcomes and winning is one key to controlling anger. You also need to recognise that you are choosing to respond to what happens with anger rather than directing your focus into your performance. Standing still and deep breathing will help to let go of anger, but you need to be gentle on yourself when you don't do what you think you should. You are never going to play perfectly and you need to accept that and learn to enjoy what you do well.

13

Beyond Fear

Fear, fear, fear... the greatest challenge to any player! Fear may be experienced directly as a feeling in your body or what is more difficult to detect is the fact that players will put boundaries in place to protect themselves from the feeling of fear.

Fear is a natural human emotion that is designed to alert us to something that may threaten us. In the good old caveman days when our physical survival was threatened by sabre tooth tigers and the like, a basic, instinctive and automatic response of fear was necessary for our survival because it triggered our fight or flight response. Whilst our Neanderthal days are long since gone, our response to the threat of danger isn't. Now, with our more sophisticated brain functioning, the perception of threat we experience is not just to our physical survival, but also to our ego, our status, our lifestyle, our identity, our success and so on. In this respect, not only do we respond to a threat that we experience with our senses; that we see or hear or touch, but we also respond to a threat, generated by our own thinking!

The main problem players have in detecting fear is that it doesn't always present itself as a feeling. Fear can present itself as an objection to change or as resistance to doing something, e.g. not doing something in competition that you can do in training. It will also present when a player "reverts to old behaviours" in the heat of the battle, as when a player becomes defensive having been playing aggressively or changes their game style when what they were doing was successful.

Fear manifests in many varied behaviours, including losing to players you should easily beat, not expressing yourself on court in competition, not raising your awareness to your contribution to your results, not taking ownership and not speaking your truth. One major impact of fear is that it paralyses performance. This is why players need to identify what it is that they are afraid of. They need to start being open, aware and honest with themselves about what frightens them. A strange thing happens when we are honest about our fears... they have less power over us. Denial of fear will only result in players simply putting in place barriers that will prevent them from feeling the fear, as opposed to addressing what caused the fear. They will stay well within their comfort zone and that means failing to achieve peak performance.

To be able to achieve your highest potential in the game, you need to learn to embrace the feeling of fear and work though it. This means accepting the uncertainty that goes with doing something for the first time. You cannot know the outcome, but if you can do it in practice then the only thing stopping you from doing it in a tournament is YOU!

Imagine this... You are facing match point against someone you had close games against before and their rating is about the same as yours. You need to beat them to be selected for the County Cup. The selectors are watching, it's been a tough match with close games every time. You know this could be your last chance to win, or you could face a tie break and you just lost the last tie break. You can feel the feeling rise up in your stomach, the tension in your shoulders growing and you just want to get it over and done with. Fear is now riding on your shoulders. If you allow the feelings to dominate your body it is doubtful whether you can make the serve under this amount of pressure. If you back yourself now, control the feelings with your deep breathing and focus your entire attention on making the best service you can, then you are feeling the fear and doing it anyway.

Here's another scenario. You have been practicing well and the technical changes you have made on your service are coming together. You have a big tournament coming up and you really want to win. You start playing in the tournament and your new serve isn't holding up that well. You hit a couple of good ones but then it lets you down again. Your old serve is still getting you some results. If you revert to your old serve you are bowing under the pressure of fear and your transition to the new serve will take longer. If you back yourself, focus on making the best of your new service, you are feeling the fear and doing it anyway.

In both cases, you may question whether you will get the results you want by carrying on with your new changes and the answer is, you simply can't know. You can't know what the results will be, it isn't possible to know. But what you do know is that, when you back yourself and go for it, you are overcoming a significant barrier to you achieving your highest potential...fear.

And when you overcome fear then your performances will feel stronger, your improvements will happen more quickly, and your results will be better.

Start by recognising the subtle nature of fear, the blocks and resistance you have to certain things in your game, maybe it's a drill you don't like or you feel you can't do something. Any resistance is a sign that you are being pushed out of your comfort zone and that makes you feel uncomfortable. Subtle, but it is still a manifestation of fear. You are likely to have a good number of reasons to back your resistance to things too! It will be very easy for you to justify not moving and staying the same. That is a trick of your mind to protect you from the discomfort. The only way is to feel the fear and carry on doing what you haven't done before; pushing yourself beyond the limits you thought existed. It takes bravery and courage, but you can do it if you really want to.

Fear can be felt physically. It can be present even when you resist and put barriers in place to stop you feeling bad. Fear will always hold you back in your performance if you let it. Become aware of the more subtle forms of fear; resistance and barriers. You need to embrace fear and then go with the challenge that is presented. You need to do things that feel uncomfortable to you. If you're not as successful as you would have liked, you can at least say that you pushed yourself.

14

The Destructive Ego

In becoming aware of your ego and its influence on your performance, I want you to understand ego as "possessed by thought". The need to understand and give labels to our experience is our ego's need to be able to define "I"; who "I" am and where "I" fit in. In our ego's striving to become more intelligent and knowledgeable we lose wisdom, joy, love and creativity. In thinking about your ego, please be aware that we all have ego and ego is neither good nor bad. It is an energetic force in us that, depending on how it is directed, will have different consequences.

It is, of course, necessary for us to use words to be able to communicate with each other, but the words we use are the surface level of an extremely complex structure of our experience. The words we use cannot possibly capture the depth of our experience and yet we can easily buy into them and become obsessed with the labels that we attach to things, and subsequently to ourselves; to our sense of "I", "me", "mine" and who I am. It is as if the words we use provide a level of security, safety and belonging, which is extremely important to us.

Our use of the words "I" and "me" are however an illusion of identity. In other words we are seeing who we are through these labels, possessions, and in our sense of ownership of something rather than seeing ourselves beyond the labels. This illusion of identity is the ego energy in action. Our illusion of self then becomes the reference point for any interpretations of our performance, experiences, thought processes and analyses; essentially, our illusion of self becomes our reality. And that reality is what influences our performance, but it is not true, it is simply a function of our ego.

For example, if you think you are a lousy grass court player you will assess your performance in accordance with your illusion of your identity as a lousy player on grass. It is like looking through a specific set of lenses. When you change the lenses you will change what you are able to see. What you will be missing is that you are far more than that. Your performance is not you, it is something you have done at a point in time, but you are much more than your performance on grass.

Our use of the word "mine" is an illusion of possession, which means that when we no longer have that thing, or it is damaged in some way, we experience the sensation of loss. This is also the ego in action. A simple example is this. A player's rating/ranking may be an illusion of possession (it is mine) and for some players can also be an illusion of identity (I am) too. Attachment to titles is the ego's illusion of possession. Even as players improve they can at points in time experience a sense of loss; loss of security, comfort, confidence etc. This happens because there are new expectations of you. If you succeed at something, improve your rating etc, you may have to do different things to maintain your place and improve further. There may be new pressures on you to perform in a certain way. Therefore, your old and comfortable ways are no longer a possibility for you, so you can experience loss.

When we use the word "I", we become identified with that thing, thought and feeling. For example:

> ➢ I am a great server of the ball
>
> ➢ I am World No 1
>
> ➢ I am not good on clay
>
> ➢ I am a better player than xxx
>
> ➢ I am a professional tennis player

And so you begin to define your sense of self around these constructions of the ego; these identity statements become your concept of who you are. Then, when the thing that you identify with doesn't happen, even if it is a negative identity, you can feel a sense of loss. It is in this way that change is made more difficult, because of the influence of ego. From your ego's perspective it makes comfort zones a more appealing place to be. Please remember though that ego is neither right nor wrong, or good nor bad. It is an energetic force with consequences.

We identify with things, thoughts, beliefs, feelings, standards of performance, outcomes, roles, ratings, rankings and tournament seeding in such a way that those things we identify with become a part of who I am; they are "me". Most players are completely identified with their thoughts and the fact that they need to think! They do not separate their thoughts from who they are, instead, they are their thoughts. Their thoughts define them. In many players it is as if that constant voice in their head has taken possession of them and in fact, for the majority, they don't even feel they have any control over that inner voice. It just happens!

Many players are so identified with their thoughts and subsequent emotions that they are simply unaware of the thoughts they have. The process of de-identifying from your thoughts is the process of acting as an observer to your thoughts and feelings. Acting as an observer to your thoughts involves you feeling as if you are standing outside of yourself and watching the thoughts as they come up. As your thoughts come up you can learn to watch them pass, as if they were clouds passing in the sky. You want to be able to allow them to pass rather than fixing your attention on any one thought. In this way, you become the "awareness" or "observer" of the thoughts and feelings rather than the thought or feeling itself.

Our ego mind works through our past. It is conditioned by your past experiences, your environment, upbringing, culture and past learning. The ego consists of a structure and content. It is because the ego has a structure that means we all have an ego, since it is this structure that provides the compulsive need to shape our identity through association with various objects, thoughts, actions etc.

The content of the ego will be shaped by environmental factors and can therefore change. For example, a player wanting desperately to win an under 14's County event is no different from a professional player wanting desperately to win at Wimbledon in so far as the sense of loss that will be experienced by the player if this doesn't happen.

Where a player is identified with their results, which means they see their results as a reflection of them personally, the loss will be experienced more painfully than where a player is not identified with their results. A player who is not identified will see their performance in context, as something they have done, rather than being a reflection of them. A player who is not identified with their results will bounce back and be in great emotional and mental shape for their next game very quickly. If you are someone who experiences negative emotions in relation to your performance hours and days after the event, you are clearly identified with your results and taking it all too personally.

So what is the problem with identifying with your results? The problem lies in the fact that the ego is never satisfied, so a player who is identified with their results can also never be satisfied. Their ego is looking to the results to "enhance" their identity, to feel more powerful, to feel good about themselves. Unfortunately, trying to find your self-worth through your results doesn't work.

Ego satisfaction is very short lived and the desire to achieve more means that it is impossible to truly feel good about yourself through your results as you can never do well enough. Of course, this drive can be erroneously thought of as a great asset for a player as it also provides a form of motivation. However, it is an illusion as a form of motivation because ego based motivation, which we all do, is based on our inherent vulnerability and our need to feel worthy. It is linked with you feeling the need to prove, justify and validate yourself. You will never be able to satisfy your need to prove yourself, since your ego will be constantly striving to feel more satisfied.

Ego identification creates an obsessive attachment to things, thoughts, feelings and behaviours. Superstition is driven by ego. A player may have superstitious behaviours (I am not referring to routine or rituals here which are an important part of the game). The player may believe that if they wear a certain shirt it will bring them good fortune or that they have to eat the same thing before every game. In these cases the ego has become identified with such behaviours and actions as a way to feel strong and secure. But problems arise quickly when the lucky shirt you wear doesn't work, or the food that you need to eat isn't available at a venue.

Many players change their equipment to give their game a boost; changing a racket or buying new trainers, or wearing designer clothing. Kids are particularly vulnerable to such ego identified behaviours and the advertising agencies are of course excellent at exploiting our human weakness, which is the ego. We all know that changing rackets, shoes and clothing will not make us a world class player, but we will at least feel good for a while; that is our ego in action.

The structure of British Tennis feeds egoic behaviour with the prevalence of status, superiority and hierarchy based systems. The ratings and ranking systems feed egoic behaviour. To get a grip on ego, means not buying into these systems as a way of developing one's sense of self.

Tennis is something you choose to do, it is not who you are. Developing a strong sense of self that is not identified with the game of tennis will enable you to achieve your highest potential because you will operate from high levels of self-esteem and confidence; you are not relying on your performance to feel good about yourself. Tennis can then become the pleasure and personal challenge that it should be rather than the fight for ego dominance that in most cases it still is.

The key to getting a grip on your ego is to become more self aware. To observe your thoughts and recognise that your thoughts, results or whatever else you identify with is not you. You become the observer of those things and in doing so begin to tame the egoic tiger that resides in each and every one of us. You need to see yourself as good enough already, not needing to prove to anyone or gain status or superiority over someone else. You cannot buy your success, you earn it through the effort you put in and even then you don't own it! Does this mean you won't feel competitive? No, on the contrary, your competitive nature will still be there and it will be founded on a more healthy motivation than your ego based desire ever could be. You will feel more fulfilled, confident and at ease with your game and your results. You will be more accepting of what happens and you will enjoy the true challenge of competing. Competing with yourself to be the best you can be.

As you work through the personal challenges in this book so you will be taking action to tame your ego's influence and developing yourself to achieve a higher level of mental and energetic functioning. The result of which will be your peak performance.

Remind yourself that you cannot truly own or possess anything. When you leave this world you can take nothing with you. If you can learn to let it go now, you will feel free to be the best that you can be, rather than being defined by your possessions, titles, successes and finances. When you become identified with things it is easy to experience significant loss. When you are less identified it is easier for you to be more accepting of change. Remind yourself that you are a wonderful human being, you have nothing to prove to anyone. Build your self-esteem by being true to yourself rather than through your ego's identification with things.

15

The Energetic
Forces of Nature

In this final chapter of Section 2, I want to introduce you to your energetic self from the archetypal perspective. The concept of archetypes comes, not least, from the extensive work of psychologist Carl Jung. An archetype is described as a collectively inherited unconscious idea, pattern of thought, image etc, universally present in individual psyches. Archetypes are very real energetic forces to us. Most people would recognise archetypes as roles, for example, mother, father, coach and child. You may be someone who is currently both a mother and a coach in which case you would adopt the patterns of thought and behaviours associated with both roles at various times in your life. Of course we have all been children too, so we know what it is like to be a child. We can easily step into and operate from the patterns of the child at any time in our life, irrespective of our current age and so it is not linked to being a child right now! A "tennis player" is also an archetype and it is a subset of the broader archetype of "athlete".

There are literally thousands of archetypal patterns and you will consistently follow the patterns of a small number of archetypes during your life. The archetypal patterns you follow make up your psychic sense of self. You may be able to think of some of your main patterns, such as mother, father, coach etc. If you are interested in finding out more about your archetypal influences then please go to my website, the details of which are given at the end of the book.

I am going to introduce you to the 4 main archetypes that we all have in common. It is important that you recognise the impact of these 4 since they provide the greatest challenge to us in developing our sense of self-esteem and self-worth. As we develop our sense of self-esteem and self-worth, so we can become less ego dominated. Players who fail to get to grips with these 4 archetypal forces will never achieve their highest potential, since they will be dominated more by fear than their desire to succeed.

FATE & DESTINY

One reason a player can never achieve their full potential unless they learn to deal with these 4 forces, is that in not dealing with them you will always take the path of least resistance. I call taking the path of least resistance as leaving things up to "fate". Fate is when you put the responsibility for your performance into the hands of others. With fate you will always take the option that creates the least amount of discomfort and you will only make changes at the pace you feel comfortable and safe, which generally means slowly. When you work with these archetypal forces and take an alternative path, which involves greater risks in life you are designing your "destiny". Following your destiny, means you overcoming the challenges that you face and always leads to you achieving peak performance. The choice that we make, to follow fate or design our destiny is the power these 4 archetypal forces have and that is why you need to become familiar with how they operate within you. When you become familiar with how they are operating within you, then you can choose which route to follow; the one of fate, or the one of destiny.

Fate then is what happens to you when you cave under fear. The decisions you take are made on the basis that you put the power of your life into the hands of others, such as coaches, parents, and even the tennis system, because you want to be taken care of; you want to feel safe. Or because you fear the consequences of making a choice that would take you to the next level in your performance, because that change could disturb the safety net that you have created for yourself and around you. As a result you will compromise the impulses to be your best because of what others would say. Fear of criticism! One thing for you to remember is this. Nobody was born hoping that you will win the tournament, or be a better player than them. Neither were you born wanting someone else to win the tournament or be a better player than you!

Parents and coaches - be aware that you will find it really hard to support the success of someone else if you do not support your own success.

Destiny, then, is taking the route of the unknown, the high risk option, without any guarantees of success. It's about making the changes you need to make because it could lead you to greater success. It's about overcoming the fear that your life will change if you are more successful, and it's about doing that even though your results are not guaranteed. This is the unknown, high risk, no guarantees, option that has the potential for the greatest level of achievement.

As we move into the world of archetypes and look at their impact on your performance, we are moving to a higher level of appreciation of the forces that each of us as human beings has to learn to manage through the course of our existence here on earth. Let's begin our journey into archetypes by looking at the shadow and light side of archetypes and the four key archetypal patterns that significantly impact a player's progression and development. They are the child, prostitute, victim and saboteur archetypes.

SHADOW & LIGHT

Each archetype has a shadow and a light side. When you are operating out of the light side of an archetype you are fully aware of your thought patterns, actions and behaviours and the consequences and the motivations that underpin each of them. You are essentially acting with a higher level of personal awareness and with consideration of your impact in a wider, universal sense. The light side and shadow side of any archetype are said to be neither positive nor negative because they are both energetic forces and as such they are neutral. However, when you are operating your life through the light side there are positive consequences for yourself and others and when you are operating out of your shadow there can be negative consequences for you and for others.

The shadow aspect of an archetype represents those aspects of your thinking, behaviour, and yourself that you are unaware of. It can be hidden from your awareness though fear or simply because until now you didn't know it existed. You'll begin to recognise when a shadow archetypal force is in operation when you hear yourself say things like: "I don't know why I get angry when I make mistakes", "I don't know why I play defensively, but", "I don't know why I continued to play that way when...", "I don't know why I changed my game when I was already winning".

Whilst you remain in this "I don't know why" state of existence, in your shadow, then you are seriously limiting your ability to improve. But if I then ask you to go into your shadow and find out what was going on and why you took, or didn't take, the actions you did, in your discovery, you would be coming into the light of that specific aspect of the archetype. Once you become aware and come into the light, you free yourself up to achieve your peak performance.

Your shadow can manifest in your motivation or in the reasons you give for your behaviour. Any reasons and motivations for your actions that are based on something negative, such as fear are likely to be shadow. For example, if your motivation to beat a player is to be able to get one over on them or feel superior, then you are operating through your shadow. If your reason for not changing your forehand grip is because you don't know how your new grip will work, then you are working through your shadow.

Fear and shadow go together. When we are behaving out of fear, we will enter into the shadow of an archetype. Moreover, if your "survival" is threatened, whether physically, emotionally, psychologically or egoically, then you will defer to behaving out of the shadow of one or more of the four key archetypes.

Becoming self-aware is moving into the light. With awareness you can change, without it you cannot. Shadow and fear are linked so to move into the light requires that you overcome your fears and be brave.

Let's look at each of the 4 archetypes in turn and explore their impact on your tennis performance.

THE CHILD ARCHETYPE

Everybody has a child archetypal force that they are influence by and through. You may or may not be aware of when you are operating out of your child archetype. The following will be things you have experienced that would indicate you are operating out of your child archetype:

> ➢ personally wounded or betrayed
> ➢ that your needs are not being met
> ➢ you need to be looked after
> ➢ feeling alone and isolated

> ➤   blaming

> ➤   playful and innocent

> ➤   trusting of others

> ➤   independent and strong

You will of course at different times in your life experience both the shadow and light side of the child archetype. Your actual physical age does not have any bearing on the expression of this archetype. Older players experience their child just as easily and often as younger players.

The main lesson of the child archetype, that is to say the thing that players have to get to grips with inside themselves, is "personal responsibility". The lesson is about learning to become responsible in this world. Players taking responsibility for their game and their contribution to the sport will become stronger and achieve better results than the player who does not deal well with this energetic force.

A player, who does not deal with their child archetype and therefore operates out of its shadow, will defer to needing to be taken care of by others; they will find excuses for their poor results and want to blame others too. The key is to become aware of when your child is taking control of your game and to get a grip of it at that time. If you find yourself blaming others for your results, or blaming something outside of you like the court conditions, then you need to remind yourself of your contribution to your results. Stop blaming things outside of yourself. Control yourself to get a better control of the game and your results.

Let's be honest, every one of us would rather be taken care of by someone else than take responsibility for ourselves. Yet responsibility is a fundamental task for our maturation. Innocence is another fundamental task that is of the child archetype, which is also essential to our maturation. Responsibility and innocence go together in the sense that innocence is about trust. I am talking about that sense of trust and innocence that we see in a child, before it learns not to trust the outside world.

Therefore, you need to trust in where you are going and that you can achieve what you want. Then, take responsibility for your results and take the action that is needed to get you there. Play with the innocence of a young child, the pure joy of playing the game and being fully engaged in that process rather than getting too hung up on your results and outcomes.

Becoming personally responsible is the lesson we all need to learn. Trust in where you are going with the innocence of a child and play the game with the joy of a child. Don't get hung up on your results and avoid blaming things outside of you for your performance.

THE PROSTITUTE ARCHETYPE

The next archetype that is very strong in all of us is the prostitute. Now, by next I don't mean to imply an order. All 4 of these archetypes work together. Obviously the child is the oldest force that we are familiar with, but the prostitute is a really powerful energetic force in us too. The prostitute's lesson for us is about not selling your soul for fear of your safety in the physical world. It's essentially about coming into your personal power. The light side of the prostitute is essentially about you recognising when you are selling yourself short so that you can stop and stand up for your true worth.

Every time you achieve something at the next level in your game, someone will come along to see if they can throw you off balance. They will test you to see if you will negotiate or undermine your success. Whether that's through criticism or some other form of pressure, they will test you to see if you will undermine your success to feel safe. An example would be this; you win against a player you should not on paper have beaten and you put it down to luck or the fact that they had a bad day. You may even tell them so after the match has ended. You are prostituting yourself by undermining your achievement.

So the main lesson of the prostitute archetype is learning not to sell your success because you are terrified for your safety. By selling your success, what I mean is undermining your results, your creativity, your opinion, selling your silence, or your wisdom, or compromising your integrity. What I mean by security is; because you are terrified to lose something or someone, or you fear you won't fit in and will feel isolated. There are some small and very significant ways that I have seen where players sell their success for safety:

> ➢ undermining your success for fear of alienating others

> ➢ not saying what you truly want from your coach or parents

- accepting criticism from others when you feel it is unjust, without saying how you feel

- having other players bully you or not standing up for yourself

- not expressing yourself on court – responding to the other players' game rather than playing your own game

- calling bad line calls because your opponent has and you want to get even

- sticking to your game even though it doesn't work and a change is necessary

- feeling tied into certain sponsorships or coaching contracts that you feel are no longer working for you

You will recognise the shadow of this archetype because when you are undermining yourself you will start to feel frustrated or irritated with yourself or others. You will begin to feel uncomfortable. Moving into the light of your prostitute archetype is therefore about first becoming aware that you are selling yourself short and then learning to speak your truth, and by your truth I also mean you recognising how good you are rather than all your failings.

The message is simple. If something bothers you, it's time to move on, change it, do what you want to do and what you believe is right for you. Speaking your truth can also be something along the lines of… "If I don't follow through with this tennis talent that I have then I will suffer, and that's the truth".

The prostitute in you is about what you are prepared to compromise or "sell out" to stay safe, and by safe here I mean physical, emotional, psychological, and egoic safety. Fear of upsetting someone or losing them as a friend is one of the main ways a player, especially female players can prostitute their development in tennis.

Most girls by their biological nature will be more inclined to forming relationships with others, therefore when it comes to competing against friends they can easily prostitute themselves so as to not negatively impact their friendships. Boys will also prostitute themselves in order to maintain the hierarchy that they function within, so as to fit in.

Being true to yourself and not compromising your success for safety is essential to developing your self-esteem and your performance. Doing things to please others and not following what you know to be the right thing for you is compromising your self. Back yourself and don't sell yourself short.

A classic example of this shadow prostitute in action, which I have seen in far too many cases of junior tennis, is our young player who cheats by calling poor line calls in order to secure a win. The player undermines himself for the purpose of winning! It is never satisfactory to cheat in order to win at any level of our being and yet they will continue this behaviour because the fear of losing is such a dominant force. They are essentially selling their self-esteem just to win. They are compromising their self-esteem, because the act of cheating to win is unacceptable and deep down every player knows that and they know when they are cheating. The fact that they still cheat, because they are desperate to win, is the shadow aspect of their prostitute archetype.

THE SABOTEUR ARCHETYPE

The third archetypal pattern is that of the saboteur. Now the saboteur's force in you is not to sabotage you, but its lesson is about your personal empowerment. The light side of the saboteur is again you recognising when you are sabotaging yourself so you can stop.

We are afraid of our own power. We are afraid of the consequences of becoming powerful because we know that our world will change. We are afraid of that change and more significantly, the uncertainty that change brings. We are afraid of what we may lose as a result of that change. And this force will act out in us even though what we are currently doing does not work for us. The consequences of change are more terrifying to us than the fact that what we are doing isn't getting us where we want to go. So we will stick with the known rather than go with the unknown.

Our saboteur is there to raise our awareness of when we are about to sabotage ourselves; for example, the pressure point in a tournament when we defer to our old way of doing things rather than go with the new technique or plan. Coaches and parents will be able to detect the saboteur in a player if they talk to them about their game and ask the question "why did you do that"? The answer will come "I don't know". When a player says "I don't know", they are likely to be operating through the shadow of their saboteur archetype.

Equally, when you ask a player "what could you have done differently" and they respond with "I don't know", their saboteur is the likely dominating force. In other words, they are not allowing themselves to become aware of why they, for example, changed the way they were playing the game when they were in the lead (something that many young players do), or that they could have attacked the other player's backhand more often. Also, if a player does give an answer to the question that doesn't quite make sense to you as a coach (because doesn't reflect your agreed plan for the game or it sounds like an excuse), this is another indicator of the saboteur and a lack of awareness on the part of the player.

The process of raising your awareness to the nature of this energetic force will enable you to prevent your saboteur from taking over and destroying your game. Another indicator that the player is not dealing with this energetic force is when they do not stick to what they need to do to be successful. Some examples are: not doing a routine of training in the gym to build strength and conditioning, not sticking to a game plan, not maintaining a new grip during match play and not sticking to your routines.

When a player does not stick to doing something that they know will improve their game, they are effectively self-sabotaging. They are not becoming aware of this force and instead will come up with a number of "reasons" (which are excuses by the way) as to why they couldn't do what they needed to do, or they may, as often happens, not even know why they didn't do it. To overcome this force requires discipline and a focus on performance objectives. The objectives give the player focus and the discipline is required to carry out the objectives even when you are feeling the shadow of the saboteur which would have you revert to your old less successful behaviour.

Players can experience this energetic force during a match in the following way. You will be playing and you will hear a voice in your head that says you should do something in the game, perhaps play more to their backhand or serve with more width, or attack the ball early. You will hear this voice and maybe get a feeling of anxiety in your solar plexus and you will not follow the instructions you have just received for fear that it may not work. You will go against your instincts, because of your anxiety about the uncertainty of the result, and you might even, subsequently, hear yourself say, "I should have done that (whatever that is for you)".

Players will often sabotage themselves in this way because they feel anxious and uncertain. Under pressure it is easy to revert to what feels safe and that will always be your old pattern, even though your new pattern might give you better results. It is worth remembering that, the anxiety you experience at the thought of doing something that may not come off is not as painful as not going with your instincts and losing anyway! And ultimately you cannot blame anyone else for this. You are getting the signal as to what you need to do and you are sabotaging it. No-one else; just you!

Another example is when you have ideas that come to you, and we are not just talking tennis here, ideas will come to you of things you would love to do or achieve and if you put a halt on those ideas because you say to yourself, I could never do that, or I don't know how, you are self sabotaging.

Self-sabotage is simply not backing yourself. You know exactly why you don't take the action you need to in order to improve aspects of your game. When we go deep inside ourselves and answer the question through our heart we all know why we don't take the action we need to. Maybe you can't be bothered to put the effort in without the guarantees. Maybe it's because it would be too painful to work that hard and still fail. Maybe it's because you don't truly believe you can make it. Maybe you are not that interested in the sport and only doing it because you have a talent and others think you are good at it, or maybe you are doing it to please your parents rather than yourself.

Deep down inside you will know exactly why you are sabotaging yourself and to not be honest with yourself can only lead to unhappiness, dissatisfaction and will negatively impact your confidence. If you are still saying you don't know after reading this book, I urge you to read it again and pay particular attention to the sections on needing to be right and your destructive ego.

Another form of the saboteur is this. For many players, the dream of success is what gives them their buzz. The actual achievement of that success would scare them to death. Talking and thinking about being World No. 1 or top 10, gives them such a buzz that they can live off that buzz. They hold on to the belief it may one day happen and yet they are not doing the 14 hour a day training regime they need to achieve the level of play that is going to be necessary to achieve that level of success. That is a form of addiction, addicted to the good feelings you get thinking about being successful. But in truth you are going nowhere. What you have to do to deal with your saboteur is to start talking honestly to yourself. If you don't want to do it, say "I don't want to do it". You don't need excuses. You can simply choose not to do it! No excuses required.

The light side of the saboteur is that you become aware of when you are about to sabotage yourself and you consciously decide whether to continue to sabotage yourself or to take a different course of action. Let's imagine... it's match point and you are serving and you become aware that part of you just wants to put the ball in court rather than serve as you have done for the rest of the match. You now have a number of choices; you can either just put the ball in court or commit to serving as you have done all match. If you go with the former, you will be sabotaging your performance, but you will be doing it through choice rather than through a lack of awareness. When you do things through choice you have control and you are taking ownership of your actions. When you remain unaware that you have a choice and just act you can always blame something or someone. Be responsible for your choices and your self-esteem will become stronger. Every time you take action to do this you are beating the shadow side of your saboteur.

Embrace uncertainty and overcome the fear that is holding you back from being the best you can be. Raise your awareness to when you are sabotaging yourself and choose a more empowering response.

THE VICTIM ARCHETYPE

The fourth archetypal force is that of the victim and its fundamental lesson for us is about boundaries. Boundaries are about you managing your own behaviour, keeping your personal energy in and healthy and not allowing others to harm your sense of self. It's about you becoming victorious in overcoming the obstacles that you face in life rather than remaining a victim of the things that happen.

You cannot always change what happens outside of you, or even if you become ill or injured, but you can certainly control how you respond to what happens. Your response is always a choice, although for deeply ingrained patterns of response it might not feel like it.

A player who overcomes injury and goes on to achieve great performances is a player who is becoming victorious over adversity. A player who changes their game by hitting wider margins to deal with a player who gives them bad line calls, rather than allowing the cheat to wind them up is becoming victorious.

A player who executes his game and works to dominate and control the game rather than responding to the opponent is becoming victorious. To overcome the shadow influence of the victim archetype is to not let anything stand in your way. Whatever obstacles you face in achieving your goal in tennis you ask yourself... "How can I overcome this? How can I get through this?" If you use your negative experience as an excuse for your poor results or performance, you are operating out of the shadow side of the victim. You are allowing yourself to be the victim of circumstances. You are effectively giving your power over to the things that happen outside of you rather than rising to the challenge and becoming victorious.

Now, please do not be deceived by how difficult it is to put these boundaries in place and overcome your victim energy. We grow up initially without any boundaries and have to learn what boundaries to put in place and how to do that. We also learn that if we put boundaries in place others may be offended, so we don't and we can leave ourselves exposed as a result.

Some boundaries that players would do well to consider are "thinking boundaries". A good thinking boundary to put in place is to not judge yourself or your opponent. By judgment I mean to say that someone or something is better or worse, stronger or weaker, good or bad, right or wrong etc. When a player takes judgment out of their game they become free to play with instinct rather than the mental act of analysis and criticism.

Judgments are often made of others because the person "threatens" us in some way; physically, emotionally, status, energetically, psychologically. A player will make judgments about how another player is playing, how strong they are, whether they can beat them or not, and yet all these judgments are mind activities that get in the way of a player playing with their heart and instincts. If you have already made a judgment that your opponent is much stronger than you and that you are unlikely to beat them; when they come on court and underperform, you are unlikely to take advantage of that fact because you have judged them to be better than you. You will become mentally fixed and not take the many opportunities that are presented during the game.

If you play free from judgment you will play your best and you will play whatever game shows up on the court. You will face the game that is present on that day, rather than the reputation, rating, or other criteria that your judgments are based on. When you play free from judgment, you are playing in the present moment, with your mind, body and energy in the same place. When you play with judgment your mind is in the past whilst your body is in the present. With your mind and body in the same place you will experience being in the "zone" and you will always achieve better results.

Don't become a victim of circumstances. Ask yourself, "how can I overcome this" and then go for it. Check your thinking boundaries are helping rather than hindering your game. Think in ways that support what you want to achieve rather than undermining yourself.

So, you have now been introduced to the 4 main archetypes that will have a strong influence on you achieving your highest potential in tennis and your life in general. These 4 archetypes can all be present at the same time, or one or two may be more dominant than the others. Your task is to identify and become aware of when you are being dominated by the shadow of these archetypes and take conscious action to overcome them. In that way you can take ownership of yourself and your behaviours.

When you overcome your shadow archetypes you stop blaming others and you take your power back. You develop a strong sense of spirit. You no longer give your power over to your opponent, or the weather, or the courts, or your coach, or your parents or anything else that is outside of you. Even if you still choose to sabotage or prostitute your performance you will be doing it with self-awareness rather than in ignorance. In that way you will feel more empowered because you are choosing how you respond. You are taking ownership and responsibility for yourself rather than resorting to blame and excuses.

Also be aware that the task of dealing with your archetypal forces is essentially about you overcoming your fears: fear of responsibility, fear of you becoming more powerful and the fear of loss that may come if you allow your world to change. You must allow your world and your game to change and trust that you will handle the consequences of that change.

SECTION
Three

Playing
Winning Tennis

Introduction

In this final section of the book we will look at a number of aspects of your psyche and how they apply to your performance. You may have chosen to read this section on its own or you may have elected to read from start to finish. Either is fine, but if you want to understand why something is as I have stated you may need to refer back to the first two sections to get a more complete appreciation of why you do what you do and why some things are difficult to change.

We start by looking at why goal setting doesn't work. Many players have tried goal setting and many have failed to use goal setting to their advantage, instead feeling demoralised and a failure. The reasons this can happen are explained here and in the penultimate chapter you are provided with a simple process for you to follow to ensure that you set goals to work for you. This penultimate chapter will change your perspective on goal setting, helping you to embrace the idea of adopting a performance focus and showing you how to use performance objectives in training and when competing.

Between these two chapters is all that you need to know to apply your mind and energy to playing peak performance tennis. You will be introduced to the pains of perfectionism and expectations and how they more often than not negatively impact your performance. You will also discover what it means to focus on the right things and how to use your focus to relax effectively? Distractions are one of the biggest hindrances to performance and knowing what to focus on and when can help you stay in the game longer. We look at the power of nerves and the power of relaxation and how to use them both in the game to your advantage. Then we move on to the power of your self-talk and how to start building a powerful self-image and developing strong positive beliefs that support your game.

Understanding motivation and memory, are next. It is essential to understand your motivation style because it is your driving force. Equally your memories are linked to your emotions and how you create your memories significantly impacts your confidence. These chapters are followed by an in depth look at confidence, which is a critical aspect of development for every tennis player. We explore what contributes to your confidence, how you can easily undermine your confidence, how to build confidence and how to remain confident under pressure even in the face of defeat.

Imagery & Shadowing is the next chapter. Imagery is important because it is through imagery that you give meaning to your experiences. Imagery is powerfully used to enhance performance and rehearse success. Learning to do imagery effectively will speed up your development and help you to overcome barriers to your success. This is followed by a short chapter on commitment and what it really means to be committed in the game. Self-evaluation follows and this is critical to your success because you need to learn how to give yourself effective feedback to build your self-confidence and self-esteem rather than destroy it. The chapter on training to perform is about how you can effectively build into your training programme skills that enable you to perform and compete. Many players play better in training than in competition and this is because they do not train to compete. We then look at fear of failure and fear of success and what you need to do to overcome fear. This is followed by the chapter on consistency and routines, which are critical for any tennis player. Many players have physical routines but very few are doing the right things mentally, this chapter shows you how you can build powerful mental routines into your game to create consistency in your performance.

Waking up in the game is essentially about mental preparation to perform and how to make best advantage of your warm up before the match. I challenge you to think of your game as a life style in the chapter on game face or life style and this is followed by the chapter on goal setting that works. Finally there is a short chapter on your formula for success. Each of the chapters can be read in isolation should you wish to simply remind yourself of something specific and of course anything you do will be linked in some way to something else so you can also read the whole section from start to finish.

16

Why Goal Setting Doesn't Work

Goal setting is usually one of the first things that a player will discuss with their mental game coach and possibly also their technical coach. Goals are considered an important part of the game because they can be used to measure success and motivate players to improve their game. However, goal setting is not as simple a process as it is often made out to be. You may be someone who has set goals in the past and achieved them and you may also have set goals and failed to achieve them. So why does goal setting not always work? There are a number of reasons which we will go through below, the first of which is the idea that goals need to be realistic and achievable.

Realistic and achievable are two words that are often misinterpreted in any discussion about goal setting. What do we mean when we talk about realistic and achievable? Is it realistic and achievable for a young player to want to be world number 1? Is it realistic and achievable for a player aged 10 just starting the game to become world number 1? Is it realistic and achievable for a 15 year old just starting tennis to make a living at the game?

You will have your own answers to the scenarios above and so will the tennis establishments, tennis coaches, strength and conditioning coaches, psychologists, other players and parents. People are very quick to determine whether a player has the ability to "make it" and I am not saying that those opinions are incorrect, but what is true is that the views of those people will strongly influence the chances of any player to realise their ambition. It is true that tennis is fundamentally a young persons sport for many reasons, not least, physical stamina and conditioning. But when decisions are made as to what is realistic and achievable for any young player that decision will effectively determine their outcome at an energetic level. This means that for a player to override the decision taken by others, they will have to have a very strong will, and an exceptionally strong support group, as well as exceptional talent.

I am privileged to work with many young tennis players who have aspirations to be the best in the world or to achieve a top 50 world ranking and on talking to their parents, it is clear that the support they are getting is fundamentally financial. Their parents don't believe they will really make it, perhaps because it would be too painful for them to believe their son or daughter could make it and then watch them fail – after all they would then be wrong! And I must say here that parents are always doing their best. They would I am sure love their young player to be successful and deep down inside want that for them, but they also have a strong need to protect their young player from being let down (which of course can be counter productive to development) and that protection can manifest in an attitude that reinforces that they won't make it. Such comments as; "it's going to be tough", "not many make it", "you have to be really special to make it", "you have to have exceptional talent to make it", are all comments that are considered to be "realistic" and can also easily send the message to a young player that they are not good enough.

Players limit their ability to achieve their dreams when they think of goal setting in a logical, rational way. Players who think that they have to get a certain number of wins in graded events to be "on track" to achieve their dream goal of playing and winning Wimbledon can be limiting themselves mentally. When they don't achieve the number of events they feel they should be they will consider they are failing. But the achievement of goals is not always a linear and logical process.

It is also the case that coaches who believe in their players' ability to achieve success will coach them accordingly. A coach who does not believe in their player to achieve a particular level of success will coach accordingly too. In other words, what the coach believes about the player will strongly influence how they coach the player to the extent that the player will achieve exactly what the coach thinks they will. Let's put this another way... have you ever known of a player exceeding their coaches' expectations for them? Rarely does that happen.

Instead of killing the ambition of a player early in their career, which I see happening, unintentionally, in many coach/parent/player interactions, I advocate an appropriate goal setting and performance management approach, in the penultimate chapter on making goal setting work. A performance management approach, even for younger players depersonalises the evaluation process, and enables players to maintain a level of responsibility and control over their tennis development and significantly positively impacts the development of confidence. In doing this they can work out in their own minds where they are in relation to where they want to go and whether they are prepared to continue doing what it will take to get them to their goal.

It is important for a player to realise where they are in the game, but it is also important for them to come to that realisation (accepting some guidance is also necessary) rather than have it forced upon them before they even start. Many parents have ambitions for their young players, some high, some not so high, and both are taking away control and personal choice from the player. Goal setting will not work effectively when the goals are determined by the coach, parent or other outside agency.

Goals must be determined by the player and directly related to their personal aspirations and dreams for them to be most effective. Clearly, for young players and players who significantly under-estimate their potential, coaches may need to give guidance in the goal setting process, but players should still be consulted in respect of what they think they want to achieve, and encouraged and supported in the achievement of what they want.

Another reason goal setting doesn't work is when goals are used as a fixed standards rather than being seen as a fluid process. When goals are seen as fixed then failure is experienced more often. There are many reasons for failure, including setting inappropriate goals, ineffective training to attain those goals, lack of motivation and lack of belief. When goals are set without appropriate management, monitoring and evaluation, and they are only appraised at the end of the timescale, it is easy to experience failure. If players fail often enough then they will avoid goal setting altogether, which happens in a large number of cases. Not setting goals also enables you to avoid taking responsibility. This may enable you to protect yourself from the disappointment of not doing as well as you would have liked, but without goals you can be left directionless and de-motivated for periods during your development. Under-estimating your capability is also going to negatively impact your ability to achieve your peak performance.

Some players may choose to set goals and not tell anyone. Again, this is often about personal protection on the basis that if you don't tell anyone they won't know you have failed. Fear is a dominant force in this behaviour. Sadly, in not sharing your aspirations it becomes hard to recruit people to support your ambitions, which can make it a lonely and difficult road. Inevitably, such players are unlikely to achieve the level of performance they could enjoy because their actions are based in fear. They are being held a victim of fear and sabotaging their potential.

Goal setting won't work if a player holds on to limiting beliefs about themselves or their performance and where they hold negative emotions in their game. Their negative thoughts and beliefs will act as a barrier to them carrying out the necessary work that is required for them to achieve their goals.

Goal setting and goal management is a very powerful tool if it is applied effectively. Making goal setting work for you is the topic of the penultimate chapter in this book.

17

The Pains of Perfectionism

Perfectionism is a trick of the egoic mind and whilst a perfectionist orientation is a good thing for the purpose of striving to improve and achieving the highest standards, any perfectionist tendencies during a competitive performance are likely to result in underperformance. There is an interesting cycle that I have noticed with players who have a strong perfectionist orientation. And by the way, coaches love perfectionists because they will work their socks off in training and perform really well in training. But this is how the cycle goes. You work really hard in training, striving to improve, then you compete and don't play as well as you do in training so you work even harder in training, but still underperform in competition. This cycle continues with two outcomes; dissatisfaction and lowered confidence.

Players with a strong perfectionist orientation generally experience more sadness in relation to their performance and because they are not getting the results they feel they deserve based on their training, they easily begin to lose confidence. But sadly, this is a self fulfilling cycle because they come back and work even harder in training again.

You can have a desire to continuously improve without suffering the pains of perfectionism. Perfection is a concept and as such it is impossible to achieve. But this doesn't stop your ego trying to achieve it, because your ego always wants more. The pains of perfectionism come from the fact that the player feels deep down inside that they are not good enough. They are seeking the solution; "feeling good enough", through something outside of themselves, that is to say, their results. By results I am referring to the match results and the perceived "quality" of ball striking. Since you cannot have 100% control over your results in a match, because there is an opponent, the perfectionist can easily become frustrated.

Perfectionists with a strong results orientation, where winning proves they are good enough, can end up relying on their opponent to lose rather than them taking on the game to win it. The perfectionist is the person who always suffers, because they are measuring their "feeling good enough" on something that is outside of themselves; either their results or the quality of their game. They can never feel good enough because there is always something they will find to be critical about and so their confidence is affected. The perfectionist who is trying to hit the perfect quality ball every time in a match will be constantly evaluating their performance during the game, which in itself is a distraction and they are likely to get frustrated easily as they see themselves underperforming more often than not.

Now as coaches and parents, we do want players to strive to be the best that they can be. We all want to be the best that we can be. But is being the best you can be about being perfect? No, that is simply the force of your destructive ego. The crazy thing is this. If a player was perfect he would win everything all the time because to extrapolate this example, he would hit all his shots perfectly all the time. No-one could touch him. Great place to be I hear you say. And of course, as you think about it, you know that it wouldn't be that great a place to be. As a player you would soon become bored because your results would be guaranteed and the challenge in the game would be gone. You could take this example to the extreme and recognise that if everyone playing tennis was perfect then there would be no game of tennis; it simply would not be possible.

So the challenge for players with a perfectionist orientation is accepting that their competitive performance can be different every day and even within a day, and "that's OK!" A perfectionist needs to recognise that their performance is perfect every time they play (I can hear you perfectionists screeching at the idea of this), in other words you have done the best you could today with the resources you had. With different resources, such as:

> being aware that being perfect isn't what the game is about. It's about how well you recover after an error

> recognise the game is about you being your best and that is about constant improvement. If you are good enough you will be the best in the world

> accepting that your game will be different on any day

> recognising that your performance is not who you are

> knowing you are still loved no matter how you play

By accessing those new resources, which are essentially new ways of thinking and feeling about your game and yourself you can get a different result. It is in the doing of something different that you will get to achieve your peak performance.

One of the main lessons a perfectionist orientated player needs to get to grips with is trust. When performing you tend to try to control the outcome rather than play the game. You usually have a strong fear of failure, which reinforces your desire to train, but when performing can easily lead to steering or pushing at the ball, playing safe rather than expressively, and having more concern over the results than players who are less obsessed with being perfect.

Most perfectionists need to lighten up a bit too. They tend to take the game very seriously and personally. It is too much about them and their status in life rather than something they do for pleasure. Even players who make a career out of tennis can suffer at the hands of a perfectionist orientation. The fact that it is your career doesn't mean you need to take it personally. Now when I say this to players the objection comes back that if they don't do it this way it means they don't care. Of course there is no link with perfectionism and caring. I can be a non-perfectionist and still care very much. This is an erroneous link that a perfectionist has constructed through their perception and interpretation of their experience.

Perfectionists need to care more about themselves and recognise that they are already good enough. They need to become aware of the dominant force of their ego mind (which is doing the measuring) and their saboteur who is scared to death of the change that will come if they achieve greater success. And the change that most perfectionists fear is that they will (in their mind) have to work harder to achieve the next level of success. Because most perfectionists cannot achieve the level of success they aspire to, even though they are working themselves really hard, the idea that they will have to work even harder if they succeed will stop them every time. Here are a few tips for perfectionist orientated players:

1. Strive for perfection in training and then trust your game when you play competitively

2. Spend some time in training where you are not evaluating the shot you have played, and whether it was up to standard or not. This you need to do to be able to stop evaluating during the game

3. Recognise that your results are not an indication of how good you are as a person and individual results on any one day are not an indication of how good you are as a tennis player. Day to day results are simply a measure of what you did on that day. Put them into context over a period of time before judging that you are doing badly!

4. If your training performances are great then go and play the same way. You are the only one who can put pressure on yourself by expecting that you should hit the ball a certain way. Often, in a match as long as it goes in it doesn't matter how pretty it is!

5. Remember there is no failure only feedback. Learn from what you are doing and move on. Pay less attention to the specifics of your game and more attention to the overall patterns of play

18

Great Expectations!

Many players are taught to have high expectations in their game. Many parents have high expectations for their children in tennis and many coaches have high expectations for their players. We hear commentators talk about what a player's expectations would be going into a tournament, given their seeding, how they have been playing and their world ranking, among other things. But rarely do players realise the impact of what it means to have expectations and how they can work both for and most importantly against you. In talking about expectations here, I must also separate expectations from goals. Expectations are not goals and whilst goals are very useful in achieving peak performance, expectations can cause more harm than good. The difference, however, is subtle and energetic in nature.

Expectations are standards that we set for ourselves, standards that we believe we "should" achieve, based on an analysis of our recent history or expected norms, such as, a 5.1

rated player should beat a 6.1 rated player. In other words you are taking your evidence from the past, based on your results, and projecting your future performance accordingly. This is of course not an uncommon process as most players will look at their past as a reflection of what should happen in the future, except that it's a bit like moving forwards in a car whilst looking through your rear view mirror. It's an easy trap to fall into thinking that, "because I did that yesterday it means I can do this today!" Of course this can work really well if you are playing well and continue to do so. But what happens when you start playing not so well?

Whilst it may be the case that tomorrow will be like yesterday, there is no absolute certainty. When players become tied in to expectations; expecting today to be the same as yesterday, they are aligning a level of certainty to their projection. Then when they don't achieve what they expected to they feel disappointed.

Expectations provide a level of security in the expected certainty based on the player's "mental" calculation. Some players will set high expectations and others may be drawn to setting low expectations, but the result either way can be just as destructive.

With high or low expectations the result is the same; your mind switches off from playing the game too early and you make mistakes. The only difference with low expectations is that the player will at least feel that they were right; they predicted the low result! Low expectations are often a way of avoiding pain because a player will have learned that having high expectations causes them pain and so they adopt the opposite strategy, but they are one of the same problem. The problem of having expectations! In other words, the problem of expecting some form of outcome or return for the effort I am putting in. Playing with no expectations is what players need to strive towards and that means adopting more of a "see what happens today" attitude. Be aware that the cycle of expectations in Fig 6. will be happening at an unconscious level unless you become aware of it!

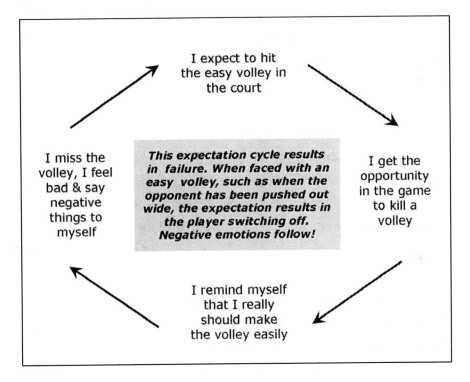

Fig 6. Expectations Process

Achieving peak performance becomes easier when players adopt no expectations. That means they go into the game with a "let's see what happens" attitude. Some players when they think of a see what happens attitude may feel that this means they don't have to put any effort into it. Here's the thing. The effort needs to go into the playing of the game rather than fighting the ego that is designed on having you work with expectations. It is the ego that will want to predict and calculate. When you play with no expectations you will experience the game as easier, because your energy is not tied up in thoughts and measurements and self criticism as you are playing. Instead your energy is directed at the playing of the game and your focus is more in the present moment. It will feel easier and this is quite scary to the ego which needs to experience things more as a fight and a struggle. Override your innate ego dominance and have no expectations. See how it goes today. Focus on performing rather than focusing on the results and enjoy the feeling and flow that follows.

Another reason for letting go of expectations is that they are bounded; they are in effect keeping you within your comfort zone. Whether you predict high or low expectations you are bounding your performance to some extent, which means that if you are out performing yourself you will self-sabotage to bring yourself in line with your expectations of yourself.

A key to identifying your expectations is in your language. The words "I should", "I must", "I have to" are all expectations in disguise. One of the ways to reframe expectations is when you hear yourself say, "I should", is to stop and say to yourself, "No, I want to, I know I can, and I will just play and see what happens today". Again, recognising that every day can be different and just because you were hitting the ball great in training doesn't mean it will happen in the match, is important.

Of course you want to carry your great training performance into the match, that is why you train, but you still have to accept that there are no guarantees and accept how you are playing on any one day. To do anything else becomes a fight and your energy is misdirected, which makes performing harder and you are less likely to achieve your best results.

Many players talk of the expectations others have of them and the pressure that this causes so it is worth mentioning this now. Firstly, remember back to how we process our experiences and recognise that technically no-one can put any pressure on you. Only you can do this to yourself as a result of your interpretation of the event or circumstances.

I don't know if parents overtly put pressure onto their children by saying "win or else", but it may happen and it can happen more subtly through phrases such as "well that was a waste of money", or "I'm not sure we can afford it". I have spoken to young players who were well aware of the financial investment their parents had made and at the time (aged 13) were not enjoying the game, but didn't feel they could stop playing because they would let their parents down. I doubt in these particular cases that their parents had directly put this pressure on their children, but it was present in their thinking none the less.

Players need to become aware of the fact that others' expectations of them are not their problem, nor their responsibility, including if those expectations come from their parents. This also means players need to get to grips with their archetypal prostitute energy, since it is this that will cause them to sell themselves short, by buying into and being controlled by others' expectations rather than being true to themselves.

Parents and coaches must look at their own motivations for investing in the player's development too. If your investment is conditional on the player achieving certain results then you are likely to be seeking your self-worth through the players outcomes, which of course cannot happen so you too will feel very disappointed. Just check on your motivations. I am not saying that you don't want players to do well, of course you do. But what I am saying is if you feel bad or feel your investment is wasted when a player doesn't achieve what you think they should, then your motivation is likely to be directed by your ego and can only lead to disappointment, which may even negatively impact your relationship with the player.

As a player, don't allow your expectations to drive or control your game. In the penultimate section I will teach you how to set effective goals so that you can adopt a healthy psychological approach to your game and let go of any destructive expectations. Learn to play with no expectations and feel that sense of peace as you play. You can still put in hard physical effort so your ego can be satisfied that you have worked hard too!

19

Focus & Concentration

Players often talk about losing concentration and my immediate response is, "where did it go then?" You cannot, not concentrate. You may not be aware of what you are concentrating on, as with daydreaming, but your attention will always be on something. Even if you were meditating your concentration/attention would be on the nothingness, the space. Your concentration must be somewhere. So when a player says that they lost concentration during a match, what they are really saying is that they allowed their concentration to move off the task of playing the game onto something else. There is a saying that is always worth remembering which is: "where your attention goes, your energy flows". I often get players to write this saying on a card and remind themselves of it during the time between games in matches. It is an absolute truth that what you give attention to you will be giving your energy to. If your attention is not on the right things in the game you are distracted. Distractions take your energy away from the game, which makes it harder to compete and give your best performance.

The terms focus and concentration are used interchangeably throughout this chapter to refer to the skill of giving your attention to something. But focus and concentration should not be forced. If a player tries to focus hard on what they are doing they are likely to experience stress and tension. The sort of focus we are looking for when playing tennis is a relaxed focus, one that is without thought, just giving your attention, observing, in the same way a tiger would focus on its prey. Its eyes would be focused and its body would be totally relaxed and poised ready to go, ready to leap.

When we focus in this relaxed way, what we can call "peripherally", two things happen. Firstly, because you are operating your vision peripherally, which is to say broadly, you will detect movement more easily and quickly and secondly, when you are in peripheral vision you activate your parasympathetic nervous system, which is that part of our central nervous system responsible for relaxation. In other words, by staying in peripheral vision you can prevent the "fight or flight" (sympathetic nervous system) response from kicking in.

Peripheral vision is being able to extend your vision to as wide a perspective as possible as demonstrated in the diagram at Fig 7. below. In adopting a wider visual perspective your vision softens and you can notice a distinct sense of relaxation between your eyes and in your temples. To do this simple technique, start by focusing your attention on a spot in front of you and then without moving your eyes at all, begin to become aware of everything that is happening in your wider visual field, to the left and right, up and down all at the same time. With practice you may even be able to sense what is happening behind you!

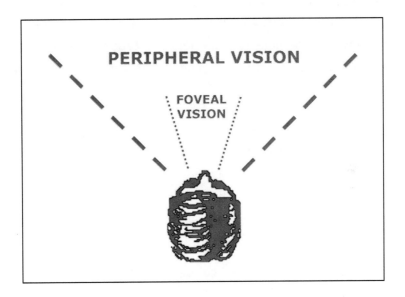

Fig 7. Peripheral & Foveal Vision

The main body of research into concentration was carried out by Robert Nideffer (www.enhanced-performance.ca), who proposed that our concentration is essentially constructed along two dimensions; breadth of attention (wide or narrow) and internal/external to self attention.

By breadth of attention we are talking about how much information you are giving your attention to. If you were in peripheral vision your breadth of attention would be wide. You would be taking account of things as far as you could see. If on the other hand you were in foveal vision, your focus would be narrow, perhaps on one thing. The easiest way to think of this is like a zoom lens on your camera. When you zoom in, you see less than when you are zoomed out.

By internal/external to self we are referring to whether you are concentrating on something outside of you, such as what is happening on the court, or something inside of you, such as how you are feeling or what you are thinking. Because of these two dimensions we are able to experience 4 types of concentration. There are, in other words, 4 places our concentration can be directed to.

1. **Broad and external to self** – such as being aware of the crowd and your coaching team, or the court in its entirety, its surface, the weather conditions and the other players actions. So this would be a broad appraisal of what you are experiencing.

2. **Broad and internal to self** – such as planning your game in your mind, criticising your performance, analysing your game, thinking about what you are going to do tomorrow or what you did last week. So this would be a broad appraisal inside your mind, your thoughts and feelings.

3. **Narrow and internal to self** – such as a specific feeling like nerves, or pain, a single thought like a trigger thought to motivate you or get you focused, mental rehearsal of a serve or shot, or attention to your breathing. So this is a narrow focus inside your mind and/or body.

4. **Narrow and external to self** – such as the service box, the line of the court, the ball, the other player serving or moving or their racket, your target (where you want the ball to go), the net, the umpire, ball boys or girls,

equipment, water bottles and even music. So these are a narrow focus and outside of you.

For each of the 4 places your concentration can be invested, there are appropriate things to be giving your attention to and inappropriate things to give your attention to. When you are playing tennis your concentration will naturally be best suited to different areas of concentration at different times during the game.

One of the keys to achieving peak performance then is to have your concentration in the most appropriate place at the most appropriate time focused on your task. So if you are going to serve the ball you might first take a broad and external perspective; you will look at the court the player and have an appreciation of the weather conditions. Then you will formulate a plan in your mind of where you want to serve the ball, which would be a broad internal focus. You will then rehearse in your mind serving the ball, maybe take a couple of deep breaths (both narrow and internal focus) and then with your attention on where you want the ball to go (narrow and external focus), you will make your serve. This would be an ideal process for a player, allowing the flow of concentration and giving their attention to the most appropriate aspects of the game during their serve.

An example of a player concentrating ineffectively could work in one of two ways; they can follow the same structure, from external and broad around the cycle to external and narrow with their attention on inappropriate (non task relevant) activities. Or they may not cycle their concentration at all; they may become stuck in one area. An example of a player who focuses on irrelevant tasks would be someone who becomes aware of the crowd (external and broad) whilst they are preparing to serve and when they step up to the line their thoughts are around what might go wrong and how they just messed the last service up (internal and broad), then they realise they feel really nervous (internal and narrow) and give their attention to that, and then they are focused on not wanting the ball to go into the net (which of course is them seeing the ball go into the net, an external and narrow focus). Of course our second player is going to get a very different result from our first, simply as a function of his concentration and focus of attention.

Fig 8. Focus

The diagram at Fig 8. above gives you some examples of appropriate and inappropriate things to focus on in tennis. You need to focus on the things that help your game rather than things that distract you and the process of changing your focus is easy. If you are distracted, simply bring your attention back to something that is relevant and helpful to your game.

Directing your attention appropriately is a discipline, but it helps if you know what to focus on when and this is where routines help. They help players focus on the right things at the right time giving them the best opportunity to execute the shot they want, although of course there are still no guarantees.

Concentration and focus can be described as a form of "trance" state. Anything that holds your attention can be described as a trance, and trance is a naturally occurring state. As a player when you are in a trance you can feel that you have not controlled it, you may experience the trance sensation as having happened to you. The "zone" state that is often referred to in all sports is in effect a trance. Some of the key indicators of trance are: Time distortion; time either moves quickly or slows down, focus of attention that absorbs the player (which could be something related to the game or not related), the amount of thought or self-talk that is happening (a positive trance will have low self-talk, a problem trance will have negative self-talk), play feels effortless in a zone trance and can feel hard work in the problem trance state. Essentially, when you are absorbed in what you are doing or thinking, whether positive or negative, you are in a trance and trance can be hard to break out from. Also, when you are in a trance state you are reinforcing your experience at an unconscious level, which means you are more likely to continue in the same vein.

So players who find that they struggle with their concentration because they cannot stop thinking about the shot, or criticising their play, or who feel anxious about playing are effectively stuck in a trance, with their focus of attention being on something negative. Within this negative trance state your mind will not be in the present moment, you will experience some of the following classic deep trance phenomena: pseudo-orientation in time as you replay the shot that you just missed in your mind, or as you think about missing your next service, or as you think of all the things you need to do to win the game. Post hypnotic suggestions as you say to yourself or believe, "I don't want to mess this up", "I always double fault on big points", "This is going to be tough", "I can't do it". Negative hallucinations (not seeing what is there) as you fail to see what you could do differently to change your outcome, and possibly even positive hallucinations (seeing what's not there) as you visualise your opponent blasting you off court with their forehand or service.

Because you are in a trance it is easy to stay there especially if you don't realise you are doing this to yourself. You could be maintaining the trance state that is preventing you from achieving your highest potential. To break the trance you first need to recognise that you have been distracted by something that is not helping your game. You then need to bring and maintain your focus of attention only on what you want to achieve right now. You can learn to control your desire to slip into common distractions like focusing on what is going wrong or all the things you will need to do to get the game back on track. Keeping your concentration in the present moment is about playing one shot at a time with both your mind and body in the same place. Whilst easy to say, I am sure you are already aware of the reasons why this can be more difficult to achieve during the game. Learning to meditate and discipline your concentration will have a positive impact on your game. For now, recognise your main distractions, pick one and commit to recognising when you slip into that distraction in the game and as you notice yourself slipping get back to something relevant for your game, even if that is as simple as focusing your attention on the ball.

20

The Power
of Nerves

Over the years players have been destroyed by nerves. Some have never even made it to the professional ranks because they were unable to control their nerves. Many young players experience nerves as something that they don't want to feel and for some, even the feeling of nerves scares them. But it is important to recognise that nerves are a necessary ingredient for performance. However, what you do need to be able to do is control and direct that nervous energy to reinforce what you want rather than to allow the feeling to debilitate you and wreck your performance. The more accomplished you become at managing and controlling your experience of nerves the greater your scope for developing your game.

In tennis, you may experience nerves at several points in the game; the start, at big points, following a mistake or number of mistakes, serving after a decision has gone against you, during tie breaks and in closing out a tight game. Your experience of nerves on each of the occasions may be different; from a mild butterfly sensation in your stomach and solar plexus area through to a tightening in your head, shoulders, arms or chest and even a complete inability to toss the ball in the air on your serve. Clearly the level of nerves you experience will impact your game, from enhancing your focus and performance through to you freezing and falling apart.

Remember that the nerves you experience are a natural fight or flight response to something that threatens you. In this case, it is your ego that is threatened by you losing the game or making errors. But you will also experience nerves based on what you are thinking at the time, and/or your beliefs around the situation in which you find yourself. So you can learn to control your nerves in several ways.

Firstly, you can work on realising that your results are not a life and death issue. Your whole world will not fall apart if you don't win the match (although for some players this is hard to believe I know), and recognise that your personal integrity is not in danger if you do not win this time. Yes you would like to win, of course, otherwise what are you doing there. You enjoy competing, so focus your attention on enjoying the moment rather than worrying about a negative outcome. Nerves remember are experienced if you feel threatened, so some of the thinking processes that will be going on, either consciously or unconsciously will be around your idea that you might not succeed, and not just that you might not succeed, but the consequences (in your mind) of not succeeding.

Secondly, as I mentioned earlier, you need to take control of your breathing, ideally before your nerves become overwhelming to you. Building deep breathing into your routines is the best way to achieve this. You do deep breathing by breathing in though your nose and out through your mouth as slowly and as deeply as you can. And you must focus all your attention on your breathing and achieving a feeling of calm, rather than allow your mind to wander back to your nerves and the underlying thought processes. You must give your attention to success and what you want to achieve rather than what you don't want to achieve.

The more you can remain in the present moment, with mind and body going in the same direction the easier it will be to control your nerves. Peripheral vision is another way to help calm your body; by getting into peripheral vision whilst you are breathing you can remain at an appropriate level of arousal for the game.

Now, clearly the game of tennis is fast moving so you might want to consider rehearsing these techniques both in training and in your mind (I will talk about using imagery later). If you are not practicing something in training (and with the mental and energetic aspects I have discussed with you here I would also add that you need to maintain your practice in your life) then don't expect to be able to tap into it when you need it during a match. Breathing techniques, especially, take dedicated practice. It is one of the simplest tools you have at your disposal and it is also one of the toughest to do properly. In fact if you are serious about your game I would recommend you take breathing lessons with someone and specifically from the meditative perspective. One of the easiest times to practice this skill is in bed when you are laying down, but also if you experience yourself feeling nervous at any time in your day to day activities, breathe. Most people when they feel nervous allow their breathing to take over and it then becomes short and shallow. If you breathe short and shallow breaths for long enough (and it doesn't need to be that long), whilst worrying about something negative happening you will be sure to induce a panic attack in yourself. You have the control and so it is up to you to exercise that control. You should also consider having breathing as part of your routines, which will then enable you to maintain your state more effectively rather than responding after the nerves have already got a grip.

21

The Higher
Power of Relaxation

Many players are afraid to relax, whether that is in the form of taking a day off from training or even having periods of their training that are focused on relaxation. We seem to have in our society an obsession with "doing" something. We have an attitude that is "I must be doing something, I must be productive otherwise I am not contributing". And, I guess the follow on from that line of thinking from the ego's perspective, is that if I am not contributing, then I am not worthy! Who knows? Check it out in yourself. Do you have to be permanently productive, active or doing things? Is it hard for you to sit down, take time out just being rather than doing? Players who struggle with relaxing are likely to experience problems if they are forced to break from the game, for example through injury or illness.

One of the reasons players don't want to take a break from the game is often linked to their limiting beliefs about how hard it will be to get back into the game. They fear they may lose their place in the ratings if they take time out. They fear that they will lose their touch and will have to work harder to get their standard back (a killer for perfectionists of course). Whatever the reason you prevent yourself from relaxing, you will be doing more harm than good.

Relaxation provides mental, emotional, physical and energetic balance. Without it players can burn out or become ill and injured or even go off of the game completely, almost as if their body has decided for them that it is time to take a break from the game. Appropriate mental and physical relaxation and rest from the game is at least as important as spending time working on your forehand or your serve.

BASIC MEDITATION

One of the best forms of relaxation is meditation and it is great for tennis players because you are training yourself in one of the key ingredients of being in the zone, that is, a quiet mind. There are many books and classes on meditation so if you are interested in pursuing it further I would advise you to check it out. Contrary to popular belief, relaxation is not achieved by watching the television. On the contrary, when you are watching television you are in a form of trance and your mind is being bombarded with messages. It is a long way from relaxation.

Meditation is a true form of relaxation that teaches you to use the power of your mind effectively. You can begin practicing meditation any time and I would advise you to start with short sessions of up to 15 minutes initially and work up to being able to spend an hour in meditation at one time. To get you started, simply sit, in the lotus position as shown in the diagram at Fig 9.

below. If you can't do that then sit with your back upright in a chair and your feet on the ground, with your hands resting on your thighs, palms upwards and your thumb touching your second finger (next to your index finger). Have your tongue touching the roof of your mouth and begin breathing in and out through your nose. Focus all your attention on your breathing.

Fig 9. Lotus Position

Do not force your breathing. Simply relax into breathing gently and easily whilst giving your attention to your breathing. If your attention wanders, which it is likely to do, then just gently bring it back to your breathing. Continue in this way throughout your meditation until you are able to do longer periods of meditation without your concentration wandering. Initially you are likely to find your concentration will wander within seconds. This is a good indication of how poorly disciplined your mind is! But with perseverance and practice you can learn to extend your sessions.

You cannot force meditation, you can only relax into it. If you try and force it you will have problems relaxing and concentrating effectively.

If you want to progress a bit further you can, whilst in meditation scan your body mentally and notice if there is any tension in any part of your body and imagine that you are breathing into that part of your body, relaxing the tension with every out breath. You should not experience pain whilst meditating, so if you do find that you are in pain at any time, stop and seek medical advice.

Remember, during the game, you will be unable to concentrate 100% of the time on the game, so don't even try. There are times in the game, such as between points, between games, during rain breaks and in some cases between matches on the same day when you need to be able to switch off. Once you are proficient at meditation this will become a much easier task for you and you will also begin to get the best out of your ability to concentrate. The end result of learning to relax during the game is that you will have more energy and your concentration will be stronger and more consistently directed appropriately; you will feel that you are "sharper" on court.

You can use meditation relaxation to experience your chakras if you want an extra challenge. You would do this by getting yourself into a good level of meditation and then concentrating on the location of each chakra from the first up your body to the seventh. You can follow the instructions below to achieve a chakra meditation. It might be useful to have someone read this out to you or record it for your use. You can also get an audio version of the meditations and other visualisation techniques off of my web site www.achievingpeakperformanceintennis.com. Be sure to leave spaces when following the chakra meditation script below to give yourself time to hold your attention for a while at each chakra centre.

CHAKRA MEDITATION

Imagine at your base chakra, at the base of your body between your legs, a small red light, bright shinning red, glowing light and breathing into that light have it expand into a big red ball of light in your first chakra. Hold your attention on that light for as long as you can and with it hold the feeling of security. Now draw your attention up to your second chakra two inches below your belly button and imagine an orange spark there. Focus your breathing on the orange spark and have it grow into a big orange ball of light, notice if the ball is spinning, you can direct it to spin if you want to. Hold your attention on that light for as long as you can and with it the feeling of power. Then move up to your solar plexus, in the centre of your body about 2 inches above your belly button and imagine a yellow dot of light there. Have that dot of light expand big and bright as the sun, glowing yellow and warming your whole body. Hold your attention there for as long as you can and with it the feeling of confidence. Now move up to your heart chakra just to the left of the centre of your chest, above your heart and notice a small green spark of light. Have that light expand and grow into a large ball of green light across your whole chest. Feel its calming and loving effects and hold your attention there for as long as you can. Now move to your throat chakra, in your throat area and imagine a blue light in your throat area. Have it grow into a ball of blue light shinning brightly. Hold your attention there for as long as you can and with it the feeling of being creative and expressing yourself. Now bring your attention to your third eye, just between your eyes and notice an indigo blue light shinning there. Focus your attention on that light and have it expand into a big indigo blue ball and focus on the light for as long as you can. Hold with it your desires and dreams. Now bring your attention to the top of your head, your crown chakra and imagine a violet light at that point. Expand that light big and bright and allow that violet light to grow into infinity connecting you to the universe. Hold in your mind the feeling of peace that you are on the right journey for you. Then you can bring your attention back to your breathing, gently in and out, and slowly allow yourself to come round to a normal waking state. As you get up and move around, do so slowly and have a good stretch before you continue with your normal activities.

22

Self-Talk

Throughout this book I have often referred to your thoughts and the impact of your thoughts on your emotional state and your performance. Those thoughts may be in your conscious mind so you are aware of them or they may be in your unconscious mind, such as your beliefs of which you might have been less aware. Self-talk is effectively your conscious thoughts. It is that voice in your head that sometimes feels as if someone else is inserting things into your mind. Whether you say your thoughts out loud or not doesn't matter, it's still your self-talk. You may experience your thoughts as if someone else is doing them to you. A bit like an alien from outer space has a direct link into your head. Of course I don't know whether that is true or not, but it is certainly very disempowering to think that someone else has put your thoughts into your head. So, since we can only assume that you put them there, then that means you can control them; you can do something with them and you can change them should you wish to.

Players will sometimes say that they cannot change their thoughts, but this is not true. What they are often referring to is the fact that the thought just appears in their head and they can't stop that from happening. But you can. Initially when you try to change your thoughts you do have the same old destructive thoughts come into your mind, since that is how you have programmed yourself. So your thoughts are likely to be a conditioned (learned) and therefore instant response. What you must do when that thought comes up is "gently" challenge it, by saying no to yourself and consciously directing your attention to something else. By repeating your new thought in your head you can begin to override your previously conditioned response.

If you can firstly become aware of repeated thoughts or things you say to yourself, such as "that was crap" whenever you hit the ball into the net, then when you hit the ball into the net, accept that you may initially get the thought come to mind, but you follow it immediately with, "no .....it wasn't deliberate, go easy on yourself", or "no, okay not what I wanted but...". Self challenge in this way, when done consistently will turn your thoughts around and at some time in the near future your old thoughts will be gone.

When players don't challenge their thoughts and self-talk it's not because they can't, it is simply that they are being lazy or have a desire to beat themselves up for not getting the result they wanted. It's as if, beating themselves up is an appropriate punishment for their crime! They are not allowing themselves to be human. It seems that making the mistake in the first place is not punishment enough! Of course in not challenging negative self-talk, it is a very quick and slippery slope to underperformance. It negatively impacts confidence and self-esteem and can easily have you feeling really down about your game.

Now, when thinking of your self-talk, I also want you to be aware of the fact that when others give you their opinion, views or feedback, if you accept what they are saying without question or challenge, you are effectively saying the same thing as they have said to yourself. In other words you are giving sanction to what they are saying and their comments become your self-talk. This means that no-one can actually influence you unless you let them; unless you give sanction to what they are saying. It is a good idea then to surround yourself with people who support what you are doing and who will encourage you to achieve your dreams rather than those people who are frightened of your success because of the impact your success will have on them.

One of the main reasons your self-talk is so important is that your mind cannot tell the difference between what you vividly imagine, with feelings, and what you experience directly with your senses. The classic example of this is your dreams. If you have ever woken up from a nightmare, sweating, with your heart racing you will know exactly what I mean. The blue eyed monster wasn't actually chasing you, yet your body (through the images in your mind) reacted is if it were happening right then and there in the flesh. But it wasn't happening, except in your mind. Your mind cannot tell the difference between what you vividly imagine and what you experience with your senses. Because your reality is held in your mind, which is great news for you it means you can change your mind and therefore change your reality. Your self-talk is one way to begin changing how you feel about your game. Of course in changing your self-talk, you may have to suspend your natural desire to self-deprecation and you will find that you need to say nice things to yourself even though you might not feel like it at the time. Keep in the back of your mind that you did not deliberately mess up and you are doing your best all the time. It just didn't work out as planned this time. There is always next time! You also need to be persistent in changing your self-talk and recognise that it will change over time.

23

Self-image

Your player self-image is critical to your success in the game of tennis. How you see yourself as a tennis player will of course be strongly influenced by how you see yourself in life, but it is possible to create for yourself a "player self-image", which I will talk about further when looking at your "game face". Here, I am more concerned with your overall self-image; how you feel about yourself as a player, what you think about yourself and how you see yourself in the tennis arena.

Your self-talk plays a significant role in the development of your self-image, as does everything else I have mentioned before this point and most of what I will mention after this point. I am sure you can see that the expectations you have of your self and your measure of success in achieving those expectations will feed into developing your self-image. How you perceive the world, your attitude to your mistakes, whether you need another's approval, what you believe to be true and how you compare yourself are all part of this self-image package.

You have the power to dictate and therefore determine your self-image. You have the power to change every aspect of what I have talked about in this book and therefore you can experience yourself however you desire. That's why it's called a self-image, only you can change it. Others cannot directly change your self-image, but you can, by giving sanction to what others say about you, allow others to influence your self-image. I would urge caution if you are the sort of player who needs a lot of external feedback about your game, that you will be strongly influenced by what others think, which can work for you if you have a positive and supportive team around you (and by this I don't mean a team that just tells you how well you are doing!), or it can work against you if you don't. In any event though, if you have a strong need for external approval you may find you have a constant battle with your confidence and self-esteem.

What I will say is this. Be gentle on yourself whilst making changes to your self-image, since change can be scary for most people. When you start changing your self-image you might initially feel a fraud and the older you are the more this can be the case; after all you have been thinking and speaking about yourself in a particular way for a very long time. How you think and feel about yourself has become your identity, therefore the work you are doing on creating your self-image is essentially about changing your identity. Remember it will be easier to feel more secure in your past and current self-image even if it is not that positive or helpful to your performance or your sense of self.

Imagine you are someone who has a reputation for coming off court and being hard on yourself, telling everyone how badly you played and you act like a joker to compensate for your disappointment. All your mates are now bought into your self concept of "critical joker" because you have been playing the role of critical joker for a long time. Now you decide you want to change so you come off court and start saying how you did really well and you are serious about wanting to improve so you cease playing the joker too. What is their response likely to be? Some will support your new self appraisal, but some may smirk or laugh at you saying "yeah come on joker".

Unintentionally, other players and people around you can keep you held to your previous reputation. This has been the case with a number of players I have worked with who struggled with anger. They ended up with a "Mr Angry" reputation that was held by their coach, other coaches, referees and tournament officials and their parents. Even during the period of time that they tried to change their behaviour, the slightest hint of anger would be picked up on, such that they were still considered to have an anger problem long after their expression of anger had shifted to similar or even less than other players. Other people would "see" their anger more than they saw the anger of other players, so a perceptual bias creeps in. This can make it hard for a player to change, but persistence does pay off. Eventually, you will be seen differently. You need to be strong through the process of change, which is why many players struggle to make the shifts necessary to change their self-image to something that supports their dream. To develop your self-image then you need to go beyond the short term and keep yourself firmly fixed on where you want to be. Your true friends will always come with you. But remember, when you change, it scares others and they will react accordingly, often in ways that try to keep you the same as you were before.

If you hold a negative or critical self-image, remember that you may be doing so because it is easier than thinking good of yourself. If you think good of yourself, you may feel you let yourself down when things don't go as you expect, so check your expectations of yourself. Can you only have a positive self-image if you are successful all the time, if you never make a mistake and win more than you lose? If your self-image is based upon your results you are likely to experience ups and downs in your self-image, you will feel positive when you are getting results and when you are not getting results your self-image will respond accordingly. This is a very shallow, destructive ego based measurement system, and something that I recommend you change in order to achieve your highest potential in the game.

Fundamentally, to change your self-image as with anything in your mental game, you need to take action. You need to act. Some ways of thinking that can help you develop your self-image are:

> ➤ Remind yourself that you are always doing your best, no matter what your results are

> ➤ Remind yourself that you are a hard worker and there is no failure, only feedback. "I got this result today, because I put these ingredients into my game today". In working out the ingredients you put into your game you will come to identify your recipe for success and can repeat it more often.

- ➢ Remind yourself that you are playing tennis because you love the game and you love the challenge

- ➢ Have a bring it on attitude to the challenges your opponent raises for you

- ➢ Give yourself permission to make mistakes recognising that you are human and no matter how many mistakes you make on any one day, you were still doing your best that day.

- ➢ Align your player image to an animal (great for younger players), such as I am a tiger player, I am a bull player, I am a bear player, I am a lion player. In this way you can align your style of play to the characteristics of the animal such as, strong, agile, fast, big, focused, alert etc.

There are a number of other ways you can create and develop your self-image that may also help you change your thinking about yourself. Clothing, accessories, hair styles, the colours you choose to wear and many other external factors can help you make the change in self-image but be aware that just changing those things alone is unlikely to have a lasting effect. You have to change how you see yourself and how you think about yourself, how you measure yourself and what you believe about yourself. Then you must take action to create the image you want.

24

The Truth
About Beliefs

Clearly the beliefs you hold about yourself as a player will
strongly influence your self-image and how you subsequently
play. But, whether you are aware of it or not, your beliefs are not
actually true. What they are though, are the rules and constructs
around which you play your game. Because you hold the belief it
becomes true for you, because you act as if it were true. Before
we look at how we do this, let's go back a stage and look at how
we form beliefs.

Remember that we perceive the world through our senses
and that every second we are bombarded with 2 million bits of
information that we filter down to about 134 bits of information
and process according to our internal filters, such as values,
language, beliefs, etc. The internal representation that we hold of
our experience then is based on only a very small amount of the
total information available to us. It is always skewed by our
personal filters. Therefore it is not a "true" reflection of what

happened, in the absolute sense. It is our perception of what happened, which makes it true for us. That means, what we believe is a function of what is experienced through each of our filters. Of course, the strongest influence on the structure of your filters and therefore your beliefs were your parents and significant others who have been involved in your upbringing, your culture and social norms.

If your father has a strong competitive nature and is very results focused, you can easily learn the same behaviours and think in the same way (or abreact and think the complete opposite, as sometimes happens). So, if your father believes that "winning is the only measure of success" then you will learn to hold the same belief. Which means that when I come along as your peak performance coach and tell you to change that belief because it can stop you achieving your highest potential in tennis as it causes you to feel more pressure, you may have some difficulty in changing it. Just because dad and you both think that "winning is the only measure of success", this does not make it true. Your beliefs are simply rules that you have learned to follow. Because you hold the belief you will act as if it is true for you. Beliefs are self fulfilling cycles. Some beliefs you hold will be very empowering and helpful in the attainment of your highest potential and some will not. Some beliefs will hold you back, and it isn't always obvious which beliefs are healthy and which are not.

Many players think it is good to hold a belief that winning is the only measure of success (and for some this may not cause them any great problems), but what does it mean when you then don't win... you are failing, and then how do you feel about that... not very happy, and then what happens? This sort of belief, whilst on the surface seems OK, and without doubt is a belief that many players hold, can lead to a wide range of problems, from low confidence through to low self-esteem; reduced effort, emotional swings and reduced motivation to play. It is of course utopian in its nature since it is not possible to win all the time; even the best players in the world lose occasionally, and during every tournament only one player comes out of it having not lost a match. The message this belief is giving to the player is that I have to win to be successful and therefore if I don't win I am a failure. If you feel a failure too often, it ceases to be a pleasure and it is then harder to achieve your highest potential.

To see how our beliefs impact our performance the chart at Fig 10. below shows the relationship between what we believe, the energy we put in, the action we take and the results we get. You will easily see the self fulfilling nature of beliefs.

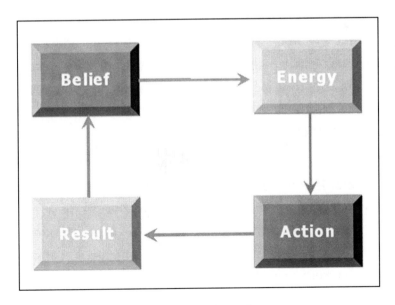

Fig 10. Beliefs Cycle

So, if I believe I can't beat someone the amount of energy and action that I put into beating them will be less than 100% and could be significantly less and so my results will reflect the amount of energy and action that I have put in too. My results will be easily less than 100%, if I get any results at all. But my belief is reinforced, so at least I can say I was right! Now, when I believe I can beat someone, the energy and action I will put in to achieving that will be significantly higher, up to 100%. My results will be significantly better than if I held the belief that I can't do it. Will I beat the player just because I believe I can and I put in 100%? Maybe, but remember there are no guarantees.

Just because you believe you can do something doesn't guarantee that your results will be 100%, but you will be assured of better results than if you believed you couldn't do it. So if you are a perfectionist orientated player who expects to get 100% if you put in 100% then unlucky! You need to address your expectations, because whilst it might happen, it is not guaranteed and you have to continue to believe and put in the energy and action without a guarantee of the results. In developing empowering and healthy beliefs for yourself it will become a positively reinforcing cycle that will enable you to achieve better results more often.

The judgments you make during your tennis career will form your beliefs. If you judge yourself as good or bad at a part of the game you will over time come to believe that to be a truth. Of course, you can continue to reinforce that through your thoughts, energy and action, or you can change it. Let's look at one way players form beliefs. A player might say to me, "I am really poor at volleying the ball". When I have asked them how much time they spend practicing their volley shots they say, "not a lot". Many players do not practice their weaker shots very often. So their effort is reflected in their performance! You can see that the belief that you are poor at the volley is only relative to the amount of effort and training that you have done. It is not a true belief, but you can maintain it as true because you are not putting in the effort. And, because you hold the belief that you are not good at the volley, you will avoid playing them in the match and if you do you are likely to perform lousy and reinforce the belief.

The original belief that you are not good at the volley was, like all beliefs, based on flawed data. Perhaps you missed some volleys in training or in a match; perhaps at a key time in a match, and then during or after the match you will have taken a decision (said to yourself) that you are not very good at the volley. The reality is simply that you missed the shots in that game, for reasons that may not even be technical! The shots may have been missed because you were mentally weak in that moment. That doesn't make you poor at volley shots, unless you chose to believe it!

I have found, as I mentioned earlier that players, especially younger players, will miss key shots such as a smash or a drive volley because they have already thought they have won the point. They have got ahead of themselves in the game. It is as if they have too much thinking time, they lose focus with the shot and mess it up. Often there is no real technical error that caused the problem, but their beliefs both in terms of their ability to play the shot, and in the belief that they have already won the point is what has caused the error.

Some key tips in identifying whether beliefs are helpful or may harm your performance are:

➢ Is your belief utopian that is to say unattainable? Positive thinking is not about setting unattainable beliefs and goals. Utopian beliefs, such as, "making mistakes means I will lose", or "you have to be perfect to be successful" do not help performance.

➢ How attached to your belief are you? If you don't achieve what you believed you would, how do you feel? If you believe that "winning is being successful" and you are constantly feeling a failure, then this belief is not helping you.

➢ The beliefs you hold about other players and how good they are (even if you think they are not very good), can easily negatively impact your performance. If you think someone is not as good as you, you can easily under perform and find yourself lowering the standard of your game to their standard. If you think someone is a lot better than you and you start winning, you may find you let your lead slip and end up losing the game.

➢ What beliefs do you hold about the courts you are playing on, the venue, the location, the tournament? Whatever beliefs you hold will influence your game. If you really love a surface, you are likely to play better than if you really hate the surface. But you need to look a little deeper. It is your hating of the surface that is causing you to play below your standard rather than the surface itself.

Learn to love every surface you play on, no matter what your experience in the past. Remember, the past is not the present and it doesn't have to be the future, but you can make it your present and future by holding on to what happened in the past.

➢ The belief that you can win (emphasis on the word can) and that you will do your best are healthy beliefs.

➢ The belief that you will get the result you deserve even though it might not be the one you want, is a very levelling belief and although you might at first not think it is particularly positive, what it is saying is that you will get the result for the ingredients you put into the game. If you want to change your results you have to change your ingredients.

➢ The best player on the day will win. What is important here is the notion of "on the day". Too many players get wrapped up with rankings and ratings and how someone played against them last time, whether someone is a cheat or not and other such distractions. The simple reality is this; the player who performs the best, across all dimensions of the game will win on that day. It doesn't mean they will win next time, later that day, tomorrow or against you next time. Go into each game with the same empowering belief that whoever performs the best will win and then focus on performing your best. There is nothing worse than losing a game and coming off knowing that if you had played even half of your own game you would have won, but because you got suckered into the opponents' antics or lucky breaks or cheating calls, you significantly under performed.

➤   Believing that you will continue to improve your game, is a healthy belief to hold, if that is what you want to do. If you don't think you can get any better and that suits you because your aspirations have changed, then of course that belief is also fine (for you).

➤   Believing that things will improve if you have a lousy start is always going to lead to better results than if you believe your game is never going to work today. And you must hold this belief with real conviction such that if your game doesn't improve you will feel somewhat surprised by the end of it. If you have a lousy start and hold the belief that things will improve, and as the game progresses and they don't improve you start to feel a little irritated, then you are not truly believing that it will improve. You are more likely to be expecting it to improve just because you believe it will and this is different. Expecting it to improve is saying that it should improve, but of course that is not the case because there are no guarantees. Your negative feeling tells you that you are not believing that your game will improve. It makes sense doesn't it? If you really believed you would improve you wouldn't feel irritated would you? You would instead feel optimistic, which is a different feeling.

➢ You have to believe before your results come, not the other way around. Your beliefs drive your performance which then drives your beliefs. So you have to start where you can. You can act as if you believe in yourself until your results come. This is a powerful form of mental strength that requires you to take action. You cannot change your beliefs though passive inaction. You can wait for your results to change, which of course they might, but your beliefs will not really have shifted unless you get consistent results over a long period of time, since as soon as your results go down hill again, your old belief will return as strong as ever.

Two powerful beliefs I would recommend you start with are:

1. **You are always doing your best.** You have to believe this no matter what your results are like and no matter what strops or frustrations you experience during your game. Essentially, whatever you are doing you are doing your best in that moment. Does it mean you are getting your best results ever? No. It means that for whatever reasons, whatever hassles you have been experiencing, whatever stresses you have bought into the game, whatever diet, sleep, exercise you have been undertaking, for all the whatever's you can think of, you are doing the best you can

in that moment in time. And of course that also means that in a different moment in time your performance can be different. Allowing for this variation in your game and accepting that you are doing your best are empowering ways to think, even if at first you don't believe them to be true.

2. **There is no failure only feedback.** Again this is a most empowering belief to hold since you can begin to look at your performance from the perspective of learning about the ingredients that made up your results. For every thing that happens in your game there are causes; there are a combination of factors that create the results therefore there is no failure, there are simply the "factors" that created the result. If you want a different result then you need to learn about the factors and change those that aren't helping. And there will be many mental factors that contribute to your results that you may have never considered before now. You are never failing. You are getting exactly the results you deserve given what you have put in. And in tennis, you are not alone. Your opponent is also contributing. But any player who comes off court and says they could have done absolutely nothing differently to change the result is, with some limited exceptions, in denial. You can always change something to make your game better, but it still doesn't guarantee you will win!

25

Motivation & Passion

If you are playing tennis it is because you are motivated to play tennis. In other words, you have some desire to play, reasons why you like to play. Maybe it's because you like the competitive nature of the game, maybe you like the social aspects, or maybe you love the winning, trophies and accolades that come with getting great results. Whatever your motivation, it is what drives you and therefore the absence of those drivers will result in a drop in your desire to play. Does this mean that some forms of motivation are better than others? Not particularly. As with everything I have talked about in this book, there is no right and wrong way of doing things, there are simply consequences of doing things a certain way. So you have a choice to either except the consequences of the way you are doing something or you can choose to change what you are doing and have different consequences.

Players will be motivated for a variety of reasons. In general when a player first starts playing the game at a young age, they just love the playing of the game, the challenge of getting the ball over the net and having the ball come back to them and then getting it over the net again is the buzz for your 5 year old. Then as players get older they come to realise that winning is prized through external rewards (including attention) and losing is not, so winning can become a significant motivational force. Then, later, in general, players progressing to professional ranks in the game will be motivated by the challenges of the game and also their successes, whether measured by titles or money. The balance of motivation between personal challenge (improvement) and outcomes (results and money) will vary from player to player and the consequences are clear. It is easy to develop measures of personal challenge and to consistently achieve new levels of performance for oneself (the personal challenge). It may be more difficult to maintain winning results and financial rewards. A player motivated by results alone is likely to come across problems when their results aren't good enough. When a player is earning a living through tennis, if they place too much emphasis on the money, their results may suffer as they will experience more pressure to do well.

Another form of motivation that is less often talked about is that people can be motivated either towards what they want or away from what they don't want. The pleasure/pain principle as it is otherwise known, is about whether someone is motivated to act to achieve pleasure or to avoid pain. This means that a player who is motivated towards what they want (pleasure) will set goals and strive towards them, pushing on as they get closer to their goal. There are very few players, in my view, who have this style of motivation. The majority of players, in part because of socialisation and biological influences, are motivated away from what they don't want (pain), which means that they will only take action when they are feeling the pain or faced with something that they don't want, such as failure.

When a player has an away from pain motivational style you are likely to see ups and downs in their performance, so they will be happy to make changes in their game if they are experiencing a problem, but they may be less motivated, or even resistant to change if things are going well for them. The impact of a player's motivational style, on their development, is significant. Any coach who has had a problem convincing a player to change their technique will relate to this. If you have a player who is reluctant to change an aspect of their game because at the moment it is going fine, yet as a coach you know it is not going to sustain them into the future, be aware that the player may need to experience the pain before they will change. The problem you have of course is that when changing they will potentially feel the pain as their results get worse before improving after the change. It is too easy for a player to associate the pain with the new change and further resist that change. You may need to start to point out all the problems with their current technique to get them to buy in to changing to something better for their future. It also helps if the player is less focused on the outcome (results) and more focused on performance factors, which I will discuss in the sections on training to perform and goal setting that works. When a player is more focused on performance factors it is easier to point out how successful they are being whilst making some significant changes to technique. A focus on results may make that success more difficult for a player to see as most technical and mental game changes can take time to translate positively into the competitive game.

It is important to understand what motivates a player to try to ensure that their motivation for the game is maintained. There are likely to be a number of reasons why a player plays and it is useful to remind yourself of the main reasons you play. It is easy to get dragged into results and become despondent, when if you dig deeper, you may find that you really enjoy the challenge more than the results. Without exception, every player I have asked whether they would prefer to win playing badly or lose playing well has said they would prefer to lose playing well. Of course they will all have different concepts of playing well, some of which may be somewhat utopian, but the point here is that winning isn't all it is made out to be. Simply, players use winning as a measure of playing well but often lose sight of the fact that it is the challenge and the exercise and all the other wonderful social aspects of playing tennis that they really enjoy. Winning is of course the icing on the cake, but it isn't the cake itself, and icing without a cake isn't much fun! Such a realisation can work wonders in putting the game into perspective and may help a player stay balanced and grounded as they progress in the game. Motivation driven by our egoic nature (winning, results, status, recognition etc) is neither right nor wrong, it simply has consequences. A balanced motivation is likely to provide better results overall and there will be much less pain along the way, but requires a particular mindset that is less ego dominated than you might be used to.

26

Memory

Your memory is a key contributor to the development of your game; it influences your beliefs, attitudes and therefore your behaviours. If you have a memory that is linked with a positive emotion you will feel positive as you recall that memory. Conversely, if you have a memory that is linked with a negative emotion you will feel negative as you recall that memory. Also, worries about future events are memories. They are future memories and can have a significant impact on your performance in the present moment.

The topic of memory is much studied and will continue to be so, since it is complex. Among psychologists it has long been known that memory is fallible, and as I am writing this book today, there is further evidence that memory is even more fallible than was first thought. The problem is that most player's think their memory is true, and when that is a positive memory, of course that is a good thing to believe, but it is not so good to believe it when it is a negative memory. One problem a player has is this; the more they recall a negative memory, the more they can reinforce its impact. The negative memory is further reinforced when you recall it or when the same thing happens in your current game. So, for example, say you played badly at a specific venue last year because your service was so lousy. This year you have been playing well, but you get to the venue and you immediately recall how you played last year (and more specifically how you feel about how you played last year). Then when you begin playing, you make a couple of service errors and the memory comes flooding back, together with the negative feelings you had back then. You are now doomed! And what is worse, you are further reinforcing your feelings towards this venue and your beliefs around your ability to play here. You have elicited in yourself the negative emotional state that you were in the last time you played so now it is a bit like digging yourself out of a pit with a teaspoon... it's possible, but tough and requires a lot of effort, including challenging your limiting beliefs.

Remember that your memory is held more strongly when there is a strong emotion linked to it, and it seems, more strongly when there is a negative emotion linked than a positive one. When a player learns to play with less negative emotion, by controlling their response to their game, they end up having fewer negative memories to recall. This makes the process of letting go of errors easier. The process of managing memory is therefore helped tremendously by players giving themselves positive feedback in their game and a more positive and objective evaluation of their performance after their game.

Memory is also state dependent, which means that the memory can be recalled more easily if you are in the same emotional and physiological state in which you experienced the memory. As an example, have you ever had someone try to cheer you up when you are miserable after a game by saying to you, "come on think of the positive shots you played"? You struggle to think of anything positive when you are feeling miserable, because positive memories are held in the state of positive and miserable memories are held in the state of miserable. But remember that emotions do pass and once the negative emotion has passed you can then think of other things.

Players who undertake their training without consideration for this link between emotion and memory are likely to be wasting a considerable amount of training time. Many players I have seen in training allow their emotions to run away with them; they train with a bad attitude, or a strop about something. They may even bring that emotion into the training venue. Players training in a poor emotional state may well be training themselves to play in that state and therefore they can teach themselves how to cope in matches with such emotions, but I wouldn't advocate this unless it is done with deliberate intention and a strategy to get you back into a positive mindset.

Most players are not training themselves to play whilst in a less than optimal emotional state; they are simply allowing their emotions to run away with them. The end result for your training could be a complete waste of time, something I am sure many coaches and players have experienced.

A poor emotional state during a training session can lead to a poor training outcome and a lousy feeling and memory of that session. This does nothing to build confidence and it doesn't help the player to develop their highest potential. It is not wrong, it simply has consequences and players must raise their awareness to their contribution to their performance and make sure that every moment counts. In my view, if a player cannot control their emotional state and their attitude during training they are better off not being there. And where squad training is concerned, not only are they influencing their own memory of the experience, they are hindering other player's in their progress too.

Future memories, commonly called worries should be replaced by more positive projected outcomes. Getting rid of the memory of bad games or shots can also assist you in letting go of poor performances. These things can be done with a visualisation technique that you can call "my coach". If past memories have significant negative emotions associated with them, then you should seek the support of a professional. The instructions to do the "my coach" technique are as follows.

When you think about the event, either a worry or a past poor play, you will be able to run that event through your mind as if running a video or movie. As you run this movie check that you are seeing yourself in the picture as if you are watching yourself on the movie screen. Now run the movie forward in slow time and when you get to a bit that you want to change. Pause the movie and see yourself making the positive changes you want. Continue running the movie and at each stage where you performed poorly, change the outcome in your mind. Once you get to the end begin the movie again and keep adjusting those aspects of your play that you are not happy with until eventually you can run the movie through and see yourself playing as you wanted to. You may need to run the movie through a number of times to get it right for you. In doing this you are essentially changing your memory for an event in a positive way.

27

Confidence

I want to firstly separate out here the concepts of confidence and self-esteem. They are not the same, although some would argue that confidence is linked to and influences self-esteem I am not convinced that this has to be true. Self-esteem is your measure of self-worth. It is a general measure of how you perceive yourself and extends way beyond your abilities in tennis. Confidence is your perception of your ability to do something. Self-efficacy is the belief that you can do something. Self-efficacy and self-confidence are considered one of the same thing for the purpose of what follows. The one common problem these terms share is that player's measure their self-esteem and self-confidence/self-efficacy based on their outcomes and successes. This is a flawed, although common, thinking pattern. It is flawed when a player only sees their success as based on their results and fails to take account of all the other great things they are doing in their game. Self-esteem is built by being true to yourself and recognising your true contribution to this world. I certainly believe that every living human being has a struggle with self-esteem, but it doesn't mean that the struggle results in poor performances or failures in life. Self-esteem and the development of it, is one of the tasks of human beings in becoming the best they can be. And for me what that means, is discovering yourself and living a life that is being true to yourself. Easier said than done! Self-confidence (confidence) then is more task or activity specific. So it will vary depending on that task and many other factors such as whether you have done it before or not, what your previous experiences were like, how much you trust yourself now, etc.

Confidence is often considered the most important aspect of mental performance and it is easy to see why this is the case. A player who is not confident is unlikely to perform well, right? Well, maybe! But most players are the only ones that undermine their confidence. Players have absolute control over their confidence and they don't realise it. Confidence is clearly very important in that it is a positive feeling usually aligned to the belief a player has in himself to be successful.

A dictionary definition of confidence is: a belief in your ability to do something. However, many players I have worked with align their confidence with a high level of certainty. In other words, they have confidence only if they believe they will be successful, either with a specific shot or in the entire match. This tends to be confidence based purely on results and it is fragile. Young players particularly will feel confident if they have assessed that they stand a good chance of winning and not so confident if they think they may lose. Because their confidence is built around their perception of their results, confidence is vulnerable and liable to go up and down in alignment with their results. Play well = feel confident and play badly = no confidence.

Great players cannot allow their confidence to be so fragile and the difference between confident versus less confident players is not in their results, it is in how they build their confidence. Great players recognise they have control over their confidence and work hard to build and maintain it.

SABOTAGING CONFIDENCE

Let's look at some of the ways in which a player sabotages their confidence.

> Seeing the negative in things rather than the positive – in changing negative thoughts about yourself and your situation consider the good things and the opportunities to do better

> Negative thoughts lead to negative emotions leads to negative behaviour and a negative self concept - negative cycle and destroys confidence

> All or none thinking - where players flit from everything working to nothing working. There is no mid-ground. It's either one extreme or another. An example of this will be players who like either very difficult drills or very easy drills, but not drills that are somewhere in the middle.

> Negative filtering - focusing only on something you perceive as negative to you, when other cues in the environment are positive. Making one double fault in your

first service game, despite winning the game, you persist in thinking about the double fault and beating yourself for it

> Emotional reasoning – you believe what you feel means something – you're feeling nervous or tense which means you will lose. Where you make links between things that are not true.

> Labelling – I have a poor smash, I have a weak serve, I lack confidence – every time something happens that supports your label you hang onto it, reinforcing your low self concept and ignoring any positive events that would challenge your negative view

> Personalisation and blame – You take everything personally and take the blame even when it is not your fault – "it's my fault I keep hitting the ball out" (even though the opponent played a shot that was difficult for you to get to)

> Over generalisation – One perceived negative event is generalised to all events – one or two missed first serves leads to generalisations about always missing your serves

> "Shoulds" and "musts" – Believing you should or must do something rather than doing it because you want to and get pleasure from it, e.g. "I should beat this person". When you don't you feel that you have let yourself down

> "Catastrophising" – making a mountain out of a molehill – one bad line call and you blow your whole game

Here are some indicators you may notice that suggest a player is struggling with their confidence:

> Doubts ("Can I play well against this person?")

> Indecision ("Should I stick to my plan or change it now?")

> Lack of trust ("I can't bring myself to swing freely through the ball in matches")

> Fear of failure ("Just get the ball in court")

> Impatience (Trying to hit the winner too early)

> Expectations (Thinking you should beat someone)

> Personalising faults ("You stupid jerk Jon, why did you do that when you know...")

BUILDING CONFIDENCE

Confidence is built as a result of how you measure and evaluate your performance, what you expect of yourself and how much you believe in your ability, irrespective of your results. Now don't get me wrong here, it is absolutely the case that getting great results is positive feedback that gives your confidence a boost, but that is very different from building your confidence based solely on your results.

The training ground is a great way to build confidence and for many players this is a wasted opportunity as the majority of players tend to just hit balls and practice technique rather than use their training to actively build confidence. The difficulty for a technical coach can be balancing the need for technical development, which is likely to result in a player's performance and therefore confidence deteriorating before it gets better, with the need to build a player's confidence. This delicate balance is helped if players are measuring their performance and improvement on factors other than just outcomes and winning.

Players generally compete all year round too, which means they like to perform well all year round. A significant proportion of training time should therefore be spent on training a player to perform confidently, which involves predominantly tactical and mental skills. Again, these elements are often not given the attention that they need and deserve in order to help a player become more than a ball hitter. For a player to become a serious competitor, they need to master their mind and not just their physical skills. Training programmes that include these elements will be helping players build confidence to perform in a way that straight forward technical training does not. In fact, in the majority of cases, straight forward technical development can be detrimental to performance because the player is constantly alerted to what they are doing wrong technically (every time they make a mistake) and spend much time trying to put it right, taking their concentration into the wrong area for performing.

Past performances are often suggested as a way of building confidence and again this is fine if you are measuring something more than results. If you just measure your results and look back at your successes, that will be fine whilst you are being successful, but not so easy if you have had a dip in performance for a while. Past performances that are just focusing on outcomes will do little to build confidence, but they will reassure you.

Many players have an idealistic, even utopian idea of confidence; they want to feel a high level of confidence all the time. Is it possible to feel 100% confident all the time? I don't know. What I do know is that if you expect that to be the case you are going to be more disappointed more often. A more powerful approach to dealing with a lack of confidence, rather than wishing you were feeling confident or even denying the fact that you don't feel confident, is accepting the fact that you feel the way you do and then going out there and just going for it anyway. In a way you need to master the skill of "acting as if" you do feel confident, or "faking it until you make it". Then your results will come and give you further reinforcement that helps you maintain your feeling of confidence. Players who hide the fact that they don't feel confident or focus on their insecurity during the game will perform worse, and that will simply reinforce their feeling of a lack of confidence.

Confidence must come before performing and that means players need to learn to build confidence on things that they have control of and can work on to improve. Building confidence requires a great deal of effort and for the most part, players will take the path of least resistance, which means that confidence only becomes a problem for them when their results are not going well. In fact, players would be advised to take care of their confidence in every session they play, training and competing. Confidence building is a proactive programme of activity in the same way that you would practice a number of drills in the perfecting of a shot.

As you look back at the list of ways in which players sabotage their confidence, you also have an easy guide as to what they need to do to build their confidence. For example, being more patient, being decisive, challenging their doubts. Each of these contributors to confidence can be managed in the training environment through appropriate drills and match play scenarios. If a player knows they can hit a cross court ball all day, they will back themselves in a game. As players learn that making a decision and sticking to it gets them better results than indecision, then they will be happier sticking to their decisions. Feedback is another critical factor in the development of confidence. Players need to be looking for what they have done well rather than being too self-critical. They need to be giving themselves reasons to feel confident rather than reasons to doubt themselves.

One of the most important factors, in building confidence, is to know what gives you confidence and what rocks your confidence. You need to identify what needs to be present for you to feel confident? And what needs to be absent for you to feel confident? If you find that you have a list that includes your results being good, no mistakes, no nerves, getting the ball in and other end result related aspects, then ask yourself if your confidence is based on you being perfect or having the perfect conditions? If this is the case then you need to do some work on recognising that you cannot be perfect and remember that your game is not a reflection of your self-esteem.

Secondly, you need to check if your confidence is based on things that you cannot control, such as the score, people watching or not watching as the case may be. If your confidence is influenced by things that you cannot control then you need to review the situation. How sensible is it for your confidence to be based on something you have no control over? Where is your power when you do that? It's not with you! Unfortunately you cannot control the score or the outcome of the game. You can only influence those things by what you do, but you cannot be entirely in control of it. That means you need to let go of trying to control things that you can't and begin to focus on the things that you can control; such as, your training programme, your emotions, how you respond to what happens, how you will respond when things don't go as you planned, that you trust yourself to do your best and so on.

The other key to building confidence is the acceptance of uncertainty, which means building your confidence based on what you know you are capable of and accepting that what may happen on any one day can be very different from that. It is that sense of knowing that you are doing your best every time even though you may not get the result you wanted. You can know that you have a strong forehand but that doesn't mean it will work as you want it to in every game you play. But you can always work hard to get the best out of your forehand on a day when it isn't perfect. Of course, the better your skills are developed the more confident you will feel. If you have technical weaknesses in your game, or shots that you cannot play or don't like playing, or you are simply not that strong at them, then don't expect to feel a high level of confidence in hitting them.

There is no easy way to build your skills, it takes effort, but building confidence doesn't require that your skills be perfect. It requires that you believe in yourself to execute your shots to the best of your ability at that time. And as a player you must recognise that your ability to execute your shots will be different at any one time, for a wide range of reasons including how well you slept and ate, what external factors are stressing you before you play, your mental approach to the game, how your opponent plays, to name a few.

Work hard at building your confidence and don't let your saboteur take over your mind or your game.

28

Imagery
& Shadowing

Shadowing is a form of imagery in which the player is physically playing the shot in slow motion without the ball; it is effectively a practice swing. Many players are encouraged to shadow shots during training as a form of rehearsal, to reinforce muscle memory for the "right" way to play the shot. Whilst the intention of shadowing on the part of the coach is both positive and valid, the execution of shadowing often leaves a lot to be desired. For shadowing to be effective and provide the returns for a player that it has the potential to deliver, it must be carried out with volition. When carried out effectively by the player it is undertaken with full concentration and it is a multi sensory experience. In other words the player feels the feelings, hears the sounds and sees the shot as if it was actually being played and uses, through the power of their mind and movement, the muscle groups for the execution of the shot. The only thing missing is the ball! Shadowing can speed up technical learning and is strongly recommended as it takes the result/outcome out of the experience and enables the player to focus on what they are doing with their swing, feet, racket etc. Shadowing can be used for a specific part of the shot, such as racket position at the back of the swing and, because it is done in slow motion, it is a great tool to link various parts of the swing together, such as feet, shoulders and racket into a full shot.

Imagery (of which shadowing is an aspect) is more broadly used to have players rehearse in their mind specific aspects of their game. You can use imagery to imagine:

- turning up at the venue and checking in
- walking out on court for the game
- warming up
- playing the game, or specific shots in the game
- overcoming errors
- coping strategies
- handling success and failure
- recovering from injuries
- goal setting
- rehearsing technical moves

It is important that players realise what is meant by the term imagery since many players I have worked with have mistakenly thought that they needed to get a technicolour, 3D image in sharp focus for it to count as imagery when this is not how most people do imagery.

Many players in fact say that they can't do imagery, but if they can describe something to you, e.g. their front door or their car or garden, they can do imagery. The quality of image each player is able to recall will be different and there are many great players who do not get strong images but instead get strong feelings. The most effective imagery is multi-sensory, so you will have a visual image, together with the feelings that you experience and the sounds that are present at the time. You would be seeing the whole thing through your own eyes, what we call associated, which means that the feelings are stronger. If you are looking at the image seeing yourself in the picture this is what we call dissociated and it may be difficult for you to experience strong emotions doing imagery this way.

Have a go now. Recall a time in the past when you were playing really well. You can run the experience through your mind as a movie, or you may just have an image of yourself at a particular time during the whole event. As you experience the image, notice if you are seeing yourself in the picture or seeing it through your own eyes. If you are seeing yourself in the picture try stepping into your shoes and seeing it through your own eyes and notice the feelings increase. You can also change the feelings by changing the size of the image, bigger or smaller (see what works for you), by making it more or less colourful, by making it clear or fuzzy, and by moving the image further away from you or closer to you. With each of the changes you make the feelings and sounds can change too. You can even add sounds to the image if you want to.

The point is that you have full control over the imagery you run in your mind. And therefore it is possible to mentally rehearse the outcome you want in your game, long before you step on court. Imagery can be used very successfully to help a player deal with nerves, slow starts, big point situations and many other aspects of the game. For those who are still not convinced that they can do imagery, just ask yourself do you worry? Do you ever go over your game in your mind after you have finished and do you focus on what went wrong? Can you remember a past event that still haunts you? That's all imagery, and you are in control of it, because you can choose what you give your attention to and what you don't. Only you can do that. Remember back to the chapter on memory and using the "my coach" technique. You can change your images and feelings about past events by changing the movie and playing it in your mind as you wanted it to happen.

If you are struggling with doing imagery, just check that you are not suffering with the human condition of needing to be right! Players I have worked with have struggled to rehearse successful outcomes to games simply because they didn't believe they would win and therefore wouldn't create a movie in their mind of them being successful. It is not that it is not possible for them to do it, it is simply that they do not want to create a movie of success for fear of it happening, or the pain that it would cause if it didn't happen. After all, if a player predicts that they can be successful and then they fail it can feel more painful. It is often easier therefore to imagine themselves not doing well.

For those who would like to use imagery more effectively in their performance, start by seeing yourself playing your shots well. Then move on to seeing yourself play the first couple of games in a match as you want to. In each of these cases rehearse only what you want, and yes it will be the perfect game. Bear in mind that in doing this mental rehearsal, it doesn't guarantee your results, but it gives you the best physiological/physical and mental chance of doing so.

One thing I would recommend all players do is to identify what might go wrong in their game and then rehearse how they will respond positively, so as to not negatively impact their game. Such mental rehearsal is called anticipation and coping. Often players will worry about something going wrong, but they don't work through in their own mind how they will respond, how they will cope and limit the damage to their game. When a player does anticipate and think through what they will do if their worst nightmare happens, in every case they respond better than if they had not thought about it. That means they get better results and do less damage to their game, and they are building both a strong memory bank and reinforcing their self-confidence.

Imagery is a hugely powerful tool and one that is certainly under or negatively utilised by the majority of amateur players. One of the main reasons for this, in my view, is the fact that the results are not always instant and not guaranteed. Players can lose faith with imagery quickly if they are sold the idea that imagery will come true. Imagery enhances your chances of executing the shots you want. Players will be doing imagery all the time; every time they re-run the movie in their mind of the shot they just missed, they are using imagery. Taking control of your imagery means not allowing your mind to run away with you and it means keeping a strong focus on what you want to achieve rather than what is going wrong.

29

Commitment

What do we mean by commitment? Training programmes and coaches often talk about player commitment and generally this is measured by the number of hours a player trains and plays. But is this really commitment? I have often asked a player whether they are giving 100% in their training and performances, which is the universally agreed measure of commitment, with a range of responses. But when I ask specific questions in respect of their mental contribution to their game, in every case, players fall short of giving 100%; they fall short of being totally committed. An example of this is the player who has an objective in his training to hit with depth, or is working on a technical aspect of his game, for example a high ball toss, only for his mind to wander to the outcome (whether the ball goes into the court) rather than staying focused on achieving his objective. Or how about the player who skips his physical session because gym work bores him, is he committed?

Commitment is about doing whatever it takes to get to your goal and many players fall a long way short of this because they have a short term focus rather than a goal focus. Commitment is also about you doing what is best for you and that requires a level of self honesty. Are you committed to you?

Often, players are too busy trying to recover their low confidence because their ego took a hammering in the last match they played. In their minds they need to see results and they need to see them now! They are not really committed to the process of developing their game of tennis, and of course developing themselves in the process. They are not truly committed to doing the bit extra that will make the difference.

Physical commitment is also much easier to demonstrate and measure than mental commitment. After all, who knows what you are thinking or concentrating on? Losing emotional control is all part of the game, because I deserve to be angry with that stupid error, right? Wrong. A player who is totally committed will work hard to maintain the most effective emotional state for them to compete. They will control their concentration and pull it back to the game when it wanders. They will recover quickly following mistakes and they will never tank a game. They will not self-sabotage because of fear. They will not sell themselves short by not being honest with how they feel.

I have seen physical tanking and I have also seen mental tanking; the latter is far more subtle, but it is clear when a player is not mentally engaged. Commitment is, for some players conditional on them getting a "fair" return on their investment and if they don't they are not interested. But this approach can never achieve your highest potential since it is driven by the logical rational measuring mind that says, "okay, I will invest this much of me and by that time I want to have gotten xy and z back". Developing your highest potential is not linear, logical, rational; and it is not fair. Developing your highest potential requires a full on commitment at every level of your game, without an expectation of a return on that investment and accompanied with a belief that you will achieve what you desire in the end. There are no guarantees remember, but you have to want it enough to give that level of commitment. Players who want it conditionally will struggle to commit themselves fully and cannot achieve their highest potential. The fact that you are not committed 100% all the time is not the main issue here. The issue is one of self honesty. I prefer players to be honest with themselves (since this is the route to self-esteem), and if they are not feeling committed, to own up to themselves that this is the case, deal with what is preventing them from committing fully and then move on.

To say you are committed when you are not fully engaging in the game or your training is only cheating yourself and denying yourself your highest potential. Commitment takes an act of bravery, and saying that you are not feeling fully committed takes courage. Courage and bravery leads to self-esteem. Saying you are committed when deep down you feel that you are not is neither brave nor courageous. You have simply allowed fear to dominate.

There is a great and well known story here to illustrate and it is called "Eggs and Bacon". What is the relationship between the chicken and the pig to your eggs and bacon at breakfast? The chicken is involved the pig is committed! I am not asking you to go so far as give your life as a sign of your commitment, but don't just be a chicken.

30

Self-Evaluation

I have talked a number of times about making sure that your self-evaluation supports you rather than brings you down. Others will always have their view of your game, your talent, your capabilities and what you can achieve in the game and it is easy to get sucked into what others think. It is of course easy because you don't have to take responsibility if someone else is saying how good you are or what you need to improve. The child archetype has a field day as it can feel protected and validated as coach and parents remind you after the game of all the great shots you played and how wonderfully you glided around the court. But, such external evaluations do not build your self-esteem and they do little for your confidence in the longer term because they leave you dependent on others to feel good about yourself. Learning to evaluate yourself positively is simple, but you must do it for it to work.

Self-evaluation starts with a decision about what to measure. If you do not decide what you want to measure about your performance you will naturally follow your perception and the results. Your perception, as you have seen, is flawed and will therefore only be a reflection of your internal filters, which means you may struggle to see the good things you have done, if for example you have a more pessimistic or perfectionist outlook. A good coach will be able to help you to decide what to measure.

Once you have decided what to measure, you need to know how you are going to measure it. During the game you cannot be thinking about how well you are doing, so you need to be able to do your evaluation at the end. If you have parents, friends or coaches watching you could have them "chart" your game for you so that you can look at your game objectively and identify the patterns in your play.

One of the best ways to give yourself positive feedback is the feedback sandwich. This is a simple technique that helps you focus on what you have done well and what you can learn from your performance. It helps you to look at your performance from a learning perspective rather than the perspective of failure and because of this it helps you to build your confidence too. If you are going to use the feedback sandwich between games make sure that it doesn't become a distraction to your playing of the game. You should only use this tool during the game if it helps you to stay positive and focused. Very simply the feedback sandwich is as follows:

➤ Come up with at least 5 things that you did really well in the match (if you are doing this between games, come up with 2 things you did really well in the game)

➤ Come up with 1 or 2 things that you learned about your game and/or yourself in the match today (again if you are doing this between games you could skip this step or come up with 1 thing)

➤ Overall identify what you did really well in the match today

➤ Finally, identify what you will do differently in the same situation next time (if between games you could skip this step. Only include it if it is not a distraction to your game)

The great thing about the feedback sandwich is that it keeps you focused on positive learnings and helps you to control your critical analytical mind, which can be so destructive to confidence. Of course the things you identify as learnings are going to come from the things that you may not have done so well, but rather than say to yourself that your forehand was rubbish, which is the sort of critical comment players might say about their game, you are instead saying, "what can I learn about the fact that my forehand was rubbish?" From this approach you may come up with a number of learnings such as:

➤ When I get tight my forehand breaks down, therefore I need to stay loose when under pressure

➤ When I am in the lead, my forehand is strong, when I was loosing I made more mistakes with it, therefore I need to work on caring less about losing and stick to making a free forehand swing

> When the game was close, my forehand margins became tighter, therefore when I am close in the game I need to maintain bigger margins

These types of learning are far more helpful than walking off court and saying my forehand was rubbish today. There will always be a reason for your game breaking down and most of the time those reasons will lie between your ears. If you can learn from what you are doing, you can make the quickest progress and you can achieve your best performances more often. If you don't take the learning from your play, you are likely to repeat the same errors over and again. As Einstein was quoted as saying, "Insanity is doing the same thing over and over again in the same way and expecting a different result".

Feedback is critical to the development of your self-esteem, confidence and motivation. Self feedback and evaluation is more powerful than being told by someone, but in order to properly evaluate yourself you need to not take things too personally. You need to adopt an observer perspective to your game and be open to the fact that you are the one who contributed to your result. You cannot put the outcome down to your opponent any more. Yes, they will have done something to influence your response, but you must look at how you responded and what your response got you. If you don't like the results you are getting, you need to change something that you are doing and to identify what to change you need to look for the learning rather than just the fault identification. Fault identification is easy, but it doesn't change things. Committing to learning from your performance and doing something differently next time will ensure you make changes in your game and therefore you will begin to change your results. Your feedback needs to be focused on what "you" will do to improve your game, and without being critical of your efforts.

Coach and parental feedback is critical to the player developing a strong internal self-evaluation system and their self-esteem. If as a coach or parent you always give feedback that reflects how you felt, such as: "I thought you played well", "I thought that was a great result", "I thought that forehand winner was awesome", you can seriously undermine the player. Whilst giving your praise is essential and will support the player, saying what you think is something different. Praising the player should be done for their contribution not just their results. In your feedback you want to be developing the player's sense of self rather than having them need you to feel good about themselves. To help you achieve this, always ask the player how they thought they did and get them to be specific about what they did well rather than simply reflecting on the outcomes. A player may build a point fantastically well and miss the final shot so praising them for the good work is healthy and keeps them focused on the task. Tell them how wonderful they are as a person irrespective of how well they play, and if you are a parent, please avoid always giving external rewards for results and remember to tell your player that you love them no matter what they do.

31

Train to Perform

Some players train, others don't. Clearly if you want to compete at higher levels in the game you will need to train. Remember, when you train, you train to make something permanent, not perfect. Therefore, the garbage in garbage out principle applies! If you are a social player the chances are that your training time is spent on the court playing friendly matches and at best taking the odd technical lesson. That's fine, just make sure you are getting the best out of your training time. It's not about training hard, it's about training smart.

Training is about more than covering the technical aspects of the game. Yes, it is important to be able to hit each of the shots in the game to achieve results, and the better you want to be the better you need to hit the ball, but there are a vast number of great ball hitters who cannot compete. In fact, there are more players that underperform than there are who over perform. Most players seeking mental game coaching can hit the ball really well in the training arena but struggle to put their skills into action in competition. They haven't been taught how to perform. And performing is a different skill set and a different mindset from training. Some attributes of the training mindset are as follows:

> ➢ Thinking about movements and components/aspects of each shot

> ➢ Your mind is more active, critical and judgmental about what you are doing

> ➢ You are striving for perfection and drilling shots to get it right

> ➢ You are trying to make it happen and likely to push hard for results

> ➢ Working and focus on technique and developing future skills

The performance mindset is pretty much the complete opposite of the training mindset and is as follows:

> ➢ Your mind is quiet - you feel absorbed in what you are doing

> ➢ You make no critical judgment about what you have done or what you need to do

> ➢ There is no technical evaluation

➢ You accept how you are playing and allow your game to happen

➢ You play the game, each shot in the moment, without regard for the past or the future

➢ You are patient for your results

The performance mindset needs to be trained. It is unlikely to just happen for a player, although players will find themselves adopting the attributes of the performance mindset if they are playing well, what might be called in a "purple patch" or in the zone. Waiting for the purple patch to happen is a slow route to success. Instead, you can set out to achieve a performance mindset. This means spending some of your training time (including when training an aspect of your technique) in the performance mindset. When playing points in training the performance mindset should be adopted, otherwise you are simply training yourself to compete with a training mindset.

Tactical training is also a significant part of training to perform since tactical thinking is the "right" sort of thinking that a player needs to do during their game. Tactics give a player something tangible to focus on achieving whilst they are playing and therefore provide a structure to their game. Even young players can follow simple tactical plans, such as hitting to the space, serving out wide and playing the ball deep. The more accomplished a player the more they will be able to vary their tactical plans and take account of their opponent. They will also learn when and how to change their plan in the game if it becomes necessary to do so.

Learning to play under pressure and handle nerves and other negative emotions are also aspects of training to compete. If you are someone who finds your training to be much less intense and less emotionally challenging than competing, then you need to build in some level of intensity into your programme. This can be done through specific drills, which your coach should be able to use with you, such as playing points out from 30:0 down, but you can also use your mind very powerfully to generate stress and intensity whilst training. Using your creative imagination you can do the following:

➤ Think of a past event when you felt really nervous, recreate that in your mind by thinking about that time so that you begin to feel the nerves, then holding on to the feeling, begin to play tennis.

➤ Start thinking of what might go wrong so that you begin to feel tight and then play. In contrast to this get yourself really loose and floppy and play – and go really loose. Make sure you do the tense version first, then the loose version and then from the loose version slowly apply a bit more tension to get to your ideal. Most players play with too much tension in their body and so the ideal you want to work towards is slightly looser than your normal level of tension.

➤ Imagine you are about to play the final point for a major tournament win; you really must make your serve count. Recreate that image in your mind until you really feel the nerves then play the point. Do this repeatedly until you are able to play well under that sort of emotional pressure.

Pushing your boundaries is about pushing your mind as well as your physical capabilities. Some players find using their mind creatively in this way feels a bit false, but as I said before it is no different from using your mind to worry about things. It is your imagination and you can use it how you choose. If you want it enough you will make sure that your training is preparing you to perform at your best. Just hitting balls is wasting training time. Muscle memory involves more than just your muscles! From an energetic perspective, your attitude and mind set will contribute at least as much to the development of your muscle memory as the number of times you hit the tennis ball.

What you focus on during training is what you will get out of it. Always remind yourself of what you are rehearsing when you are training and ask yourself, how is this going to help me to perform? If the answer is that it isn't then you need to seriously review what you are doing. And please remember that we are talking about you rehearsing your state of mind, attitude, approach to dealing with mistakes etc; all aspects of your mental game are being rehearsed when you are training. If you are slack with your mind in training, what makes you think you are going to be any more disciplined in the match? You may manage it on occasions but you will lack mental consistency and robustness and your performance will suffer accordingly.

Obviously there needs to be a balance of what is going to help you today to perform and what is going to help you in the future. Technical training will support your future and may not help you perform today; performance training will help you today. You need to ensure that you are training for both today and your future. Having confidence that your training is taking you in the direction you want to go is of critical importance. If you are not confident in your training programme you will not be confident in your performance. As a parent I would advise you to ask more questions of whoever is coaching your children to ensure that their programme of development is including training them to perform.

You can see the training and performing mindsets in the context of learning illustrated in the cycle in Fig 11. below, where a player moves from unconsciously incompetent through to unconsciously competent:

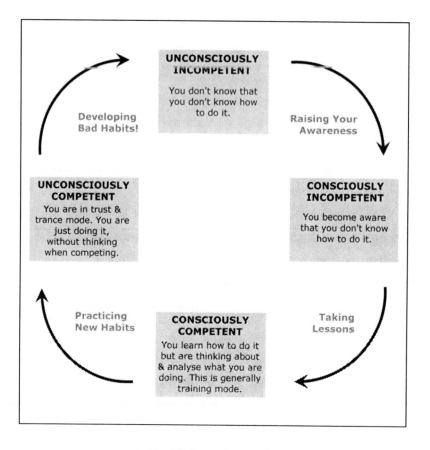

Fig 11. Learning cycle

The learning cycle above shows the progression of learning for a player for any skill in tennis, including the learning of mental skills. Initially a player will be unaware that they are incompetent (unconsciously incompetent), then through raising their awareness they can become aware that they don't know how to do something (consciously incompetent), then with lessons the player is thinking about how to do it, whilst doing it (consciously competent) and then finally when the skill is performed automatically the player is operating through unconscious competence. This is a continuous cycle of learning. The training mindset is carried out, for the most part, at the level of "conscious competence" and yet performance is best carried out at the level of "unconscious competence", which is when the player is not thinking about how to play the game (from a technical perspective). When they are unconsciously competent they are absorbed in the game and just playing, as if in a trance. Many players get stuck in the trap of playing competitive tennis through the consciously competent mind, which means they think too much about the wrong things, are over analytical and critical, often leading to physical paralysis and poor performance. If you practice during training at the level of unconscious competence, you can learn to build trust and a quiet mind, which will result in you adopting, more easily, the appropriate mind set for competing.

32

Fear of Failure
& Success

I am sure that by now you are fully aware that overcoming fear plays a significant part in the development of your mental and energetic game and in the achievement of peak performance. Fear is of course, simply, energy. Fear can have tremendous power over you if you let it. Fear can also be used to motivate players as we have seen with the away from motivation styles, whereby a player is motivated by moving away from pain; fear plays a part.

I cannot think of any player or coach or parent that I have coached, where fear is not preventing them from achieving their full potential. Parents are fearful that their children won't make it or that their children will feel bad and suffer for not achieving success. Coaches are fearful that their reputation is on the line when they are working with a player and fearful that they might not be giving the best advice, that they might in fact be giving poor advice. And players are fearful that they won't be successful, that they will be embarrassed or feel less of a person, or not fit in.

Fear of failure is a very real energy and the biggest threat to the majority of players and yet failure doesn't really exist. It is a concept. It is only because of the ego's measurement system, the comparisons with others, and the desire to be perceived of status that causes this problem. When a player begins to play from higher levels of awareness they recognise that these ego driven desires are actually not real and therefore not important. They realise that the only thing that is important is them, their personal improvement, their personal challenges and their sense of fulfilment. Such things do not come just from winning matches and trophies; they come from overcoming the human fallibilities that I have outlined throughout this book. They come from recognising the energetic forces at play and working to overcome them rather than succumbing to them. They come from recognising how you get the results that you do, taking ownership and doing whatever it takes (ethically and morally) to get what you want. They come from taking your power back, putting yourself first, building your self-esteem and recognising that there is no comparison to be made. However you play, whatever you do in the game, you are being successful for you at that point in time. It is a snapshot of your whole existence and every time you play it will be different in some way. Different is neither good nor bad from the perspective of learning. Good or bad is a judgment of the ego mind. The only failure in tennis (and life of course) is to carry on doing the same things and expecting a different result. That is insane!

Some players have said that they fear success and this is also a very real problem as I outlined in the energy section. What they fear is the change that will come with success; the changes to their relationship with others, the changes in responsibility and effort that will be required to maintain themselves at the next level are just two examples. Of course, this fear is irrational in the sense that the changes that come as a result of success are unlikely (except in the very small number of cases) to happen overnight. You will have plenty of opportunity to grow into your new elevated levels of play and you will get used to them very quickly.

My advice to players who think they struggle with a fear of success is to get them to worry about it when it happens! Whilst this may sound flippant it is not at all. Fear of success is a worry about the future, but the future may not happen so, as with any worries, don't worry about it, trust that you will know how to handle it when you get there and then leave it until you do.

It is an act of self-sabotage to allow fear of success and fear of failure to stop you achieving what you want and the only way to address your fears is to work right through them. Become aware of what your fears are about, challenge their truth and go and play anyway.

33

Consistency
& Routines

Routines in tennis are a great way to achieve a level of consistency in your approach to the game. Many players I work with think they have routines but in fact they mostly have physical routines, with no account for the mental aspects of the routine. The key to consistency is doing the same thing mentally every time, irrespective of the outcome of your previous shot.

Because, as human beings we like structure, routines are an excellent way to provide a level of psychological security and safety. They give the mind something structured to think about which enables players to stay focused on what is important rather than being distracted by things not related to the game. You will no doubt have seen how precise professional players are at the beginning of every point they play, whether serving or receiving. But have you also noticed that they follow routines between games too?

Your routines during the game start at the end of the point just played and finish as you serve or receive the next play. The routine should be the same, mentally, irrespective of how the previous point finished. The structure of a routine is not just about physical actions, such as bouncing the ball before serving. What is important is what you are doing with your mind at each stage of the routine. A simple structure of a routine is as follows:

1. Let go of the previous point (whether you won or lost it). Often players will go and pick up their towel and wipe their face, or walk to the back of the court as a trigger to letting go of the previous point. You must actively let go of the point rather than dwell on it. The easiest way to do this is to imagine how you wanted to play it and commit in your mind to doing that next time. Give yourself permission to let go of the previous point.

2. Relax, for a few seconds. This is where deep breathing comes into your routine and if you are someone who struggles with anger, standing still whilst deep breathing is a good thing to do. Players can look at racket strings and tweak them whilst relaxing, but if you need to handle anxiety, nerves or other negative emotions you are best just standing still and focusing your attention on your breathing, with your intention on being calm.

3. Refocus your attention on what you want to do in the next point (your plan if you are serving or receiving). It is

important to decide what you want to do rather than hit and hope. Be very clear in your mind where you want to serve the ball and how you want the ball to behave (with slice, or kick or flat).

4. Stay focused on your target for service (usually whilst bouncing the ball) and then serve. If you are receiving you will have your awareness on the other player so you can anticipate where they will serve to.

The mental aspects of the routine outlined above should be built into the physical routine and I have given some indicators as to how that can be done. Visualisation also comes into routines very powerfully as you are creating an image of where you want to serve or how you want to execute your tactical plan before play begins. Doing your routines consistently will lead to a more consistent performance, but you need to do your routines with commitment. If you struggle in a particular area, such as letting go of the previous shot, then you will need to do some more work on yourself to identify why making mistakes is such a big deal for you. You can build in additional aspects, for example if you have extreme nerves you can build in deep breathing after the point has finished and before you bounce the ball on service, or before you step up to the line to receive.

Ideally, you want to take the same length of time to complete the routine every time. You can use a stop watch to practice this. One of the main reasons for being precise with this is that when you are losing or playing badly, or even excitable you can easily speed up what you are doing. This can be disastrous to your game. Routines help to slow you down, calm you down and keep you focused.

Between games you need to learn to relax and this is a great time to use the technique I gave you called peripheral vision, in Chapter 19 on Focus and Concentration. Sitting for fifteen seconds just staring into space and allowing yourself to be aware (without any internal commentary) of everything that is happening at the boundaries of your awareness will enable you to switch off. Your main focus should then be on what you want to achieve in the next game; your tactical plan. Sometimes when players focus on the score they can put pressure on themselves to catch up if they are not doing so well; the "I must win the next game" self-talk can kick in. The point is that you don't really need to remind yourself that you need to win the next game, what you need to focus your attention on is how you plan to play out the next game so as to give yourself the best opportunity to win! That is different. If you are allowed a length of time between games, then take it. But make sure you follow a routine to enable you to relax and refocus. If you are sitting on the side of the court worrying about how you are playing or what the score is, you are unlikely to be able to focus effectively on doing your best in the next game.

Routines are simple and by following a mental routine consistently you can achieve a greater level of security and comfort, feel calm and deal with big points more effectively. But, you have to be disciplined. You need to make sure that you practice doing your mental routines in your training. Every time you hit a shot in training that you don't like the outcome of, you should be working your routine to let it go before you carry on the next drill. If you don't work your routines in training you shouldn't expect them to be there in your matches and especially at crunch points in your match.

You have to commit to doing your routines on every point and then you have to do them. Be aware that when you are learning to put effective routines into your game (as when you are learning to put anything into your game) you will be doing it in the state of conscious competence which means you will have to think about it for a while before you become familiar with it. When it becomes a natural process you will be doing it through unconscious competence, which means you will be doing really well.

34

Waking Up
In the Game

The title of this chapter is in fact a question. At what point do you really wake up in the game? You may be a player who carries out a warm up before you begin play, or maybe you just hit with the opponent before starting the game? Whichever type of player you are, still begs the question, when is all of you present on the court and I would also add, for how long are you on court?

There is no doubt, in our current world as we know it, that your body is always present in the moment. Your body will be on court when you are playing, but is your mind with it, or is it somewhere else? Are you playing the game with clarity of vision that feels light and easy or is it hard work, a struggle, feeling like a fight?

Waking up in the game is about mind and body being in the present moment "experiencing" and "being at one" with the game. In this state there is no fight, there are no worries, there are no critical or evaluative thought processes happening, you are simply present and playing without judgment and without commentary. If you have never tried it before, try playing a few shots without your mind giving a running commentary of what is going on, just being present and observing the game. You will probably find it tough if you are not used to having a quiet mind. If this is you, then I recommend you practice meditation. It's a fun thing to do and you will feel the stress drop from your head immediately, you will feel mentally lighter and freer.

Of course getting your mind and body at one together is the ultimate state in which you want to be playing tennis; in the zone, but achieving this state starts well before you begin playing tennis. The warm up you do will have a significant impact on your ability to get into the zone. The warm up is one of the key ingredients to your achieving peak performance. Now, because many players are social rather than professional players they don't have the same amount of time to get ready for a match. Whatever type of player you are your warm up needs to be as efficient as possible.

Most players start the game without being appropriately, mentally, warmed up. They may not quite be up for it, or they may be too up for it. They may be thinking about stresses and other things going on in their private or work life, or what they need to do after the game. If you are a tennis committee member, or team captain, there will be calls on your time that impact your tennis playing time too. But you owe it to yourself to give yourself the best opportunity to enjoy your tennis, so spending even 10 minutes getting yourself mentally present for the game will help, and your results will be better for it too. I often recommend to social players (and especially if you are on committee or even studying for exams) to stay in their car once they get to the venue for 10 minutes to unwind from the journey and all that had been happening before they arrived. If you do not have a car, find a quiet place you can be alone for 10 minutes when you get to the venue. You need to actively let go of what you brought with you to the venue and give yourself permission to give your time to your tennis.

In these 10 minutes you want to be sat quietly and allowing any thoughts that come up to pass, without fixing your attention on them. If you have been practicing meditation you will find this becomes easy to do. If anything comes up that is really important, just promise yourself that you will pick it up again after tennis and then allow it to pass. You can also do a quick body scan and notice if you are holding any tension in your body, particularly your neck and shoulders and make sure you relax them by breathing deeply into the point of tension and on the out breath release the tension.

If you are someone who has time for a full warm up, you should also include the 10 minute chill out before beginning your warm up. Your mind needs to be present for your warm up as well as your match if you are going to get the best out of your game. The physical warm up that you do is exactly that. It is for you to warm up physically and to get your hand eye coordination going. If you are not mentally engaged before you do your warm up, you may find you struggle with your hand eye coordination or with your ball control. Irregular ball flight and distance control is often a symptom of tension and you want to get that sorted before you start the game.

Most players will hit with their opponent before the game begins, running through each of the shots from ground strokes to net play, volleys, smash and service. Again, your mind needs to be present at this time, ideally without too much criticism and evaluation of what you are doing and more consideration of what you want to do with the ball.

Some players, and especially younger players, think that the warm up is the place to start to get one over on their opponent and give too much attention to trying to prove how hard they can hit the ball and not enough attention to what their own body is doing, how relaxed they are, where their concentration is etc. The hitting warm up is not the place to let your ego out! It is also not the time to make too many decisions about how you think the other person will play. The warm up is not a reflection of how the match will go and in some cases it isn't even close. Unfortunately, too many players allow their confidence to be affected by what happens in the warm up; they make decisions about their opponent and how hard they hit the ball, how big their serve is and then extrapolate how well they think the other guy will play.

Of course, the warm up is a good place to get a feel for whether your opponent has any obvious weaknesses, but be sure to remind yourself that things can change in the game.

Some key mental objectives you want to achieve in the warm up are:

➢ Do whatever it takes to let go of anything not related to tennis, before you begin to warm up

- ➢ Become aware of how your body is feeling today and release any unnecessary tension

- ➢ Sense if you are feeling nervous and use deep breathing to control your nerves

- ➢ Check what your thoughts are and make sure you are thinking only those things that will help you. If you have doubts running through your mind, challenge them. Remember, maybe you will win, maybe you won't, that is the reality of the game, but no matter what the end result, you can commit to giving yourself 100%

- ➢ Think about your game plan and how you would like to play. Rehearsing in your mind, through imagery, with all the feelings is a great way to start the game. Rehearse only the things you want to happen

- ➢ Think about one major thing that could throw you off track today and then work out what you will do if that thing happens

- ➢ Think about how you will respond if you have a good lead in the game and commit to pushing on to the end

- ➢ Spend some time relaxing before you hit with the opponent, after you have thought through your plans for the game. Switch off if you can. Music is a great way to control your emotional state; you can chill out or get yourself fired up with music. I would urge caution on the firing yourself up front, since for the majority of players their body is usually too fired up and they need to reduce adrenalin!

Remember, when you are hitting with the opponent, the game has not begun. Focus on yourself and what you want to get out of this hitting warm up to feel confident going into the game. If you finish the hitting warm up with your opponent and you are not feeling confident you need to look at what you are doing in your warm up, since you are not preparing yourself well enough. When you are psyched up, your concentration will be sharp, you will feel some mild nerves (butterfly feeling) and you will feel ready to go. If you are over psyched you may experience too much nerves and your concentration can feel tight. If you are under psyched you may experience no nerves at all and a wandering concentration. Become aware of the balance that works for you and use your warm up time, no matter how short, to get into the state that is right for your game. To not do so will provide you with a very real reason for not being successful, but deep down inside you will also know you are letting yourself down. Of course you can also accept that you have not given appropriate consideration to your warm up and then simply accept your results. Either way you will feel more content than beating yourself up for not performing when you haven't warmed up properly!

35

Game Face
or Lifestyle?

Sometimes players are taught to put on a game face for the competition, which can enable them to overcome some of the fears and anxieties they feel if they are being themselves on court. This can be a very effective way of separating yourself from your game, but for some players it might not work because even the idea of acting as if they were someone else scares or embarrasses them. It can be helpful to think of yourself as a different person on court and off court, especially if you are quiet, shy and don't like upsetting people. Young players, and especially girls, who struggle playing against their friends may find putting on a game face useful to help them overcome their anxieties.

Essentially, the game face can be applied in many ways, but what is happening is that the player is creating a boundary between their real self and their playing self. Their playing self can even become someone else; a famous player who they aspire to be like or play like. When a player adopts the character of someone else they are effectively modelling that player, therefore it is wise to select only the best players to model. When children are young (under age 7, and up to 14) they model really well, which is why (I hate to say this) they end up with the same bad habits as their parents and significant others who have influenced them! Players taught by parents will model not only what they are told, but they will model what they see, and feel. Young players model the behaviour far more easily than the instructions. A point worth being aware of when you select your coach for sure!

Adopting a game face, by modelling someone else can be easier than developing your own game face. If you are going to create your own game face you need to decide on the characteristics that you want to adopt on court and then commit to doing exactly that. Characteristics that are positive are: bravery, commitment, focused, determined to succeed, powerful, courageous, solid, confident, secure, strong, competitive and happy. This is clearly easier to achieve when things are going your way and can be more difficult when the game gets tight, but you have to be persistent. One way of committing to your game face is by having a trigger. That is, a time when you put it on and a time when you take it off and I would suggest that you put on your game face when you step into the court and take your position at the side of the court and take it off as soon as you can after the game is finished, again the court side seat (if you have a seat) provides a good trigger. If you can make the trigger the same irrespective of the venue you are playing at this will make it easier.

Having a game face is great and works really well for some players, but if you struggle, please remember all that I have shared with you in this book. You are you. The wonderful characteristics that you display on the tennis court are simply a reflection of you in your life. Therefore embodying the qualities of a peak performer means developing yourself as a person and a performer as well as a player.

If you have a fear of failure on the court you will also have a fear of failure off court. If you don't take responsibility for yourself on court you won't be doing so off court and so it goes on. The tennis court is a micro version of your inner life. Therefore, I believe that when you are changing your mental and energetic approach to your game, you are changing it in your life too. The way you use your mind and energy is a lifestyle decision. This means that your life is a great practice area for game and vice versa. What it also means is that if you continue to allow, for example, your anger to get to you in your life, don't be surprised if you struggle to control it on the court. If you are perfectionist in life, it will come out on court too. It is worth therefore checking with yourself. Is it okay for you to make the changes that you need to make to improve your game? Ask yourself what impact this will have on your life, and is that okay too?

Everything I have suggested you work on in this book will positively impact your life, will result in you feeling less stressed and getting more enjoyment out of your game and therefore your life. But only you can decide how far you are prepared to go.

36

Goal Setting
That Works

Goal setting, whether formally or informally, influences your mental processing, your energy and therefore your behaviour and results. Having goals can be very motivating providing they are set at an appropriate level. If they are not they can be very demotivating or just keep you safe without moving very far. When we set goals that we really want to achieve, we influence the way in which we delete, distort and generalise the information in our external world. We begin to see and experience things that we hadn't seen or been aware of before we set the goals. In this sense goal setting is strongly linked with the law of attraction in that you are directing your energy towards something that you want. Remember, where your attention goes your energy flows. Goals also give you something against which you can measure your progress and build your confidence. They are something you strive for as opposed to expectations which are something you already feel you should be able to do or have. Goals also help a player to identify what they need to do; what aspects of their game they need to improve, in order to achieve the dream goal itself. If you have a dream goal you can ensure it becomes a reality by charting your progress against the smaller objectives that you achieve along the way. And of course, if as a player you find that you are unable to achieve your goals or you are unwilling to put in the necessary work to improve your game, then you can always decide that your dream goal is not really what you want.

I have personally worked with a number of players, only for some of them to find that they don't really want their dream goal after all. And that's okay. It is better to find out as early as possible that you don't really want what you thought you did, rather than live on the idea of achieving something that you have no real intention of pursuing and then being disappointed for failing at the end of the day. Sometimes our ego can deceive us that we want something when deep down inside we are not prepared to give up what we would need to, in order to get it.

So before you even get to the stage of setting targets to improve your performance in the various aspects of the game; technical, tactical, physical and mental, it is worth running your dream goal through an internal checking process to see whether you really do want it. I will cover performance goals after we look at how to define your dream goal.

The goal setting process is outlined below for you to take your dream goal through. I strongly recommend that you spend at least 3 hours doing this exercise and also that you write it all out by hand. At the end of the process you should feel very clear about where you are going and whether you want the goal you thought you did. If you find that you don't want your goal any more you can run your next idea through the same process too. Remember, if you don't really want what you thought you did, you are unlikely to achieve it anyway!

DREAM GOAL PROCESS

Step One. The first step is to clearly identify where you are now. You need to describe in as much detail as possible where your game is right now; your strengths and weaknesses, your rating or ranking and do this in as much detail as you can gather. If during this time any negative thoughts come up about your game such as, "I can't", or "it's not going to happen", jot them down next to the thing you were writing when they came to your mind. So for example if you are writing down that your first service % is currently 30% and a voice in your head says, "you're just not good enough" then write that down too. The thoughts that arise during this process are indicators of what will hold you back in achieving your dream.

Step Two. The second step is to come up with a multi-sensory image of your dream goal. This means going forward in your mind to the time that you will have your dream goal. It may be 5 years or more ahead of you, but you must go to that time in your mind and create the image of you achieving your dream goal. And you need to create this image as if it were happening now. I want you to be looking through your own eyes and notice; who else is there with you? What are you doing, saying, and feeling? What smells are around? What tastes are there? Go into as much detail as you can. I had one player who wrote 8 pages of A4 describing his goal and whilst you don't need to compete with him, you do need more than a few lines. There is a simple rule here, the more detail you have of this image and the stronger the positive feelings you experience whilst you are imagining it, the more likely you will be to achieve it. It makes sense doesn't it? You are not going to work your backside off for something that doesn't make you feel great!

Now, during this process of imagining your dream goal in the future, if you experience any blockages (such as negative emotions, anxiety, or negative thoughts), you need to jot them down too. If you find yourself saying, "I would love this goal, but..." then you need to jot down all the "buts" that come up for you. Also jot down if you have an "if only" that comes up. So for example, if you are imaging your goal and saying to yourself, "that would be fantastic, if only I knew how to do..." The things that you capture are things that you are going to need to work on to free yourself to be able to see clearly what you want.

If you struggle to get a strong image of your dream goal and don't feel any positive emotions when thinking about it; maybe you feel neutral or even a bit despondent, this is an indication of a blockage in your energy system (which will also be linked to your thoughts and beliefs). This will certainly hold you back from achieving what you want. It doesn't necessarily mean that you don't want your goal. It may just mean that you are stopping yourself. The best way to recognise what is stopping you from imagining your goal is to ask yourself that question, "what is stopping me forming the image?" If you come up with the answer that "I can't..." then be aware that you are putting barriers in place. Dig deeper and you will find the thing that you need to address to free yourself up.

Many players hit blockages so please don't be put off by this process, if you really want clarity and to know that you are chasing a dream you want it is a process worth going through. You will need to be honest with yourself and it may help to work with a professional if you are struggling to do this on your own. One of the main reasons for having goal setting at the end of this book is because players are likely to need to address the "human" aspects of themselves that have been discussed in the other chapters in order to be able to write their goals effectively. In other words, any "stuff" you are holding onto will impact your ability to achieve your highest potential in the game. Your "stuff" will also hinder your ability to set not only your dream goal, but it will also impact your motivation to commit to short term goals and objectives.

In deciding on your dream goal make sure you are being very specific with your vision so that you will know that you have your goal. If you are a player who wants to win Wimbledon, you may have an image of you holding the trophy above your head as the press cameras are snapping away and the crowd cheering, for example. Seeing yourself playing in the final at Wimbledon would not be as good an image if you want to win, since the result is not known if you are in the middle of playing! Equally, if you want to be a professional tennis player, be sure to extend your goal to winning as a professional player or earning money as a professional player. Your mind will work with the images you give it. Many players have struggled once they achieved professional status simply because their goal did not extend into seeing themselves having a successful career.

When you set your goal in your mind in the way I have described you are lighting up your Reticular Activating System (RAS), which means that you will begin to see your game differently. Your RAS is like your internal radar that identifies things that will support your aspirations. You will notice things that you didn't notice before and opportunities will present themselves that you would not have been aware of before. An example of this is a player who decided that she really wanted to turn professional and within a few days, she met a man at her club who was in the business of corporate sponsorship. They got chatting and by the end of the month she was signed up to receive sponsorship to assist her on her route. Now the man had been a member of the same club as her for some years and they had even spoken before, but because she had not set her goal in her mind, she had not been aware of what he did. The process of her having her goal firmly fixed in her mind meant that she was alert to the opportunities in the external world; opportunities that had been their before but which she had filtered out!

An example of this process in action that most of you will be familiar with is in the buying of a car. If you have ever decided to buy a car, the moment at which you decide on the colour or make of the car you begin to see loads of them on the road; they were there before but you never saw them! Or one for pregnant mothers; as soon as you realise you are pregnant, or even planning pregnancy, you see far more pregnant women and small babies than you had ever noticed before. This is the power of setting out what you want and in tennis it is the power behind goal setting. Now, moving on to the next steps in the process of goal setting...

Step Three. By now you have your goal image in mind and when you think about it you should feel really great inside. The achievement of your goal makes you feel just fantastic, buzzing, and bright inside; that "on top of the world feeling". So now you can ask yourself a few more questions to check that your goal is ecological and congruent for you.

1) Ask yourself, "what will the achievement of this goal get for you or allow you to do?" This is an interesting question which can help you understand your higher motivations. So for example, if I had a goal to be earning £2million on tour by the age of 20, I might answer the question with things like: a nice house, help my family, a nice car, fame, designer clothing, I can give money to charity, etc. The money in and of itself is not a great motivator, but what you can get with money certainly can be. Of course you may also be able to get some of the things that you identify without the money and this can mean that the original goal of £2 million is not actually that important. Check out your deeper motivations for your goal. If you find that your higher motivations are to get approval, status or recognition then be careful. You must recognise that your goal may not actually achieve those things for you since they are social constructs dependent on other people!

2) Ask yourself, "is this goal just for you?" In other words is it driven by you, for you, and maintained by you? If your goal is for the benefit of someone else, then once again this is not a solid goal. Players may want to achieve goals to get approval from parents (this happens more than you may think), or approval and status from peers. The goal isn't just for them, it is to prove something. Now I am not saying that this won't work for you, but what you need to be aware of is that you can achieve anything you set out to and still not get the approval or status that you are seeking. And if that is the case you may achieve your goal and only end up feeling disappointed. Remember, people often struggle with someone else's success so don't be surprised if

your success is not received the way you expect it to be. A psychologically healthier approach is to have goals that are for your pleasure.

Also check that the goal is maintained by you. Now that doesn't mean that you can't recruit people to help you achieve your goal. You will of course need the support of a coaching team, sponsors and others. But what is important here, is that you are not reliant on one single person, such that if that person was not around you would not be able to achieve your goal. The achievement of your tennis goals must be attainable by you and not reliant on any one person, i.e. a specific coach or parent. You may need to change your support team along the way to get your goal. That does not mean that you shouldn't enjoy sharing and celebrate your success with those who are close to you.

3) You also need to ask yourself, "what am I prepared to give up in order to get my goal?" You need to understand your boundaries here. Are you the sort of player who will give up your relationship if you have to? Will you be happy leaving your family behind as you travel to play? Are you prepared to put other aspects of your life on hold to achieve what you want? These are serious questions that require a lot of consideration and will need you to go deep inside yourself. You cannot answer these questions with your mind. You need to answer them with your heart. You can even imagine (ideally in meditation) going into your heart and asking these questions and see how you feel.

4) The next question you need to ask is this, "what do I need to do to achieve my goal?" This is where you are identifying the gap between where you are now in your game and what you need to do to get to your goal. There will be some obvious things such as getting an appropriate rating/ranking, winning certain graded

tournaments, getting the right team on board with you, having the right kit and developing certain skills (physical, mental, tactical and technical). There will also be the things that you identified in steps 1 and 2 above that are holding you back that you need to deal with. There may be certain knowledge that you need to obtain. You may need to find sponsorship or other forms of funding to support you. You may need to live in a specific location for ease of training. You may even decide that you would be better training abroad. Each of the things that you come up with may also require you to do something, so they will then become sub-tasks you need to complete. Essentially, as you go through this process you will come up with a series of actions that you can then put on a time line, which gives each one a deadline. You are now developing the bones of your goal plan.

5) Now you have gone through the process ask yourself two final questions (which you may have already answered in getting this far), "what will I gain?" And, "what will I lose if I get my goal?" These are crunch questions and again take some time to go inside your heart and answer them as honestly as possible. It is easy for your mind to deceive you that you want something, but your heart will be honest with you. Make sure you look at all the things that you will lose along your journey; possibly time, friendships, socials, other activities, family, relationships? Once you have come up with your list of things you may lose then you simply have to ask yourself, am I prepared to give these things up to get my goal? If the answer is yes then great. If the answer is no, that is also great. You will be a happier person either way. And what you have done throughout this process is be very honest with yourself and identify your deepest motivations.

SHORT-TERM AND PERFORMANCE GOALS

So having set out your dream goal, you need to focus your attention on the short term goals, both for the coming 12 months and then on a daily and weekly and monthly basis. When you asked yourself what you need to do to achieve your dream goal you will have come up with a number of activities and development points that you need to achieve over a period of time. No matter how good you think you are mentally in the game, there will always be something that you can improve, that is the human dilemma; none of us is perfect, we all have our limits and therefore our potential for improvement is infinite.

Step Four. The next step is to come up with a number of goals that you would like to achieve in the coming 12 months. Initially, and most likely the first thing that will come to mind, are outcome goals, such as rating or ranking goals, winning tournaments or matches and being selected for teams. Be aware that goals such as winning and being selected for teams are not 100% in your control therefore they are not really very smart goals. After all, you can play an absolute blinder and still get beaten if the other player happens to be better on the day! Be aware that the outcome goals you set are "ideals" that you would like to achieve. Once you have set your outcome goals for the next 12 months you need to identify what you are going to do to achieve them. The things you need to do technically, tactically, mentally and physically. These things then become your performance goals. In many respects your performance goals are more important than the outcome goals. Whilst the outcome goals set your intention, it is your performance goals that drive your action on a daily basis. They are your route to your dream goal.

Performance objectives can be set monthly, weekly and daily and they enable you to keep focused on what you are doing in the present moment to get you to where you want to go in the future. One great question to ask yourself is this; "what have I done to get me closer to my goal today?" If you ask yourself this question several days in a row and come up with the answer, "nothing" then you need to review your dream goal and your performance objectives because it might be that something isn't motivating you enough?

What is important, and sometimes lacking in tennis development is a level of coherence and integration between the main elements; tactical, technical, mental and physical. Performance goals can be used to create coherence across all the developmental areas. For example, as a player are you applying your mental skills whilst undertaking your physical and technical training? If you are not that interested in your physical training and just go through the motions, you are losing valuable mental training time and holding back your progress. If you allow yourself to get frustrated when changing technical aspects to your game you are not helping your mental game. When playing points in a training game do you follow your routines and have a tactical plan, or are you just hitting balls to win points? In essence, during every aspect of your tennis development you need to take account of your mind and energy and how you are managing that part of your game. Everything you do in your training and life is a rehearsal for your performance from a mental and energetic perspective.

Performance objectives should be designed, where possible, to balance with your playing schedule, particularly where major changes are planned. For younger players it could be argued that skill development should take priority over match performance on the basis that it is more difficult to change things at a later stage in development. However, remember that from a mental and energetic perspective you are developing yourself as a person as well as a tennis player, and it is never to early to start that process. It is also important for children to play competitive tennis of some sort since they generally like the fun of competing, but this should be done with less emphasis on the results and a greater emphasis on the process of tennis. So, when playing matches young players should be encouraged to focus more on their performance (the process) than the results, with praise given for the achievement of objectives rather than just the result or outcome. There may be some people who disagree on this point but I am simply urging you to get the balance right. Too great an emphasis on results leads to players giving up this wonderful game and can easily lead to low self-esteem and low confidence. There are specific developmental guidelines available and any good tennis coach will be able to help you decide on what is appropriate at each stage.

For an older player it is more helpful to make major technical changes when you do not have a heavy competitive schedule. You also need to take account of the changes you are making in terms of your expectations for your performance. By that I don't mean having low expectations (as many players are advised to do, being told that you will struggle with something for a few months), I mean playing without any expectations and a "see what happens" attitude. The reason for this is that you can block your potential success when you think that you won't do well. Free yourself up and see how it goes, whilst feeling confident in knowing that the technical changes you are making will serve you well in time.

So, performance objectives will be set for every aspect of your game and each of your coaching team will be able to define these with you. You should set performance objectives for training and for competing. When you are working on your mental game, pick just one thing to work on at a time and pick the one thing that is going to make the biggest difference to your game now.

The same principle of working to one objective at a time should also apply to technical instruction since trying to get a player to work on several things at once is complex, confusing and more often than not results in slower progress. We can only give our attention to one thing at one time whilst working consciously because our conscious thinking happens in a linear fashion. Keeping objectives simple helps the player to stay focused on what they are trying to achieve, otherwise they will always defer to the outcome. So a player working on his footwork at the same time as his backswing and finishing the swing high on his follow through, making sure he uses his shoulders in the turn of his swing will simply measure his success on whether the ball goes in or not. He will not be attentive to any of the objectives that his coach is trying to instruct.

Please don't over evaluate how well you are doing your mental objectives whilst you are actively training, this is a distraction. Simply be aware of when you are doing your mental objectives and if you stray from doing them, bring yourself back to doing them, without beating yourself up for not doing them! Remember, over evaluation is also something that hinders performance. At the end of your training just make a note of the percentage of time you achieved your objective and try to improve on it each time you train. Some mental/energy based objectives for you to follow are:

- ➤ Deep breathing after every point (in training deep breathing can be done after every drill). You will be able to find a time between drills or aspects of drills to build this into your training. By deliberately doing deep breathing during your training at specific points in time and with your concentration on your breathing, you will be developing the discipline.

- ➤ Take something positive out of every shot you play in training and competing, no matter how small that is. It is important to reflect positively on everything you do as this is building your positive memory bank and building your confidence. There will always be something positive and if you can't initially find it, you just have to be willing to look for it beyond the result.

- ➤ Commit to giving your full concentration every time you are engaged in an activity or drill and when you are not active, chill out. You need to learn to control your concentration and not let it run away with you so you should be able to switch your attention easily from one thing to another. Every time your concentration wanders, bring it back to what you are doing. Being lazy in this area, encourages you to be lazy in the competition.

- ➤ Commit to controlling your emotions in training. If you allow yourself to get frustrated in training, you will do the same in a match. Controlling your self-talk and evaluating success through the achievement of your objectives rather than just whether the ball goes in or not, are both keys to assisting you to control your emotions.

➤ Recognise when you are sabotaging yourself and change your response to the situation. As an example, if your coach wants you to do something and you say "I can't", then (providing you have no physical problem that prevents you) you are sabotaging yourself. Turn it around by saying "how can I?" Then work on what you are being asked to do.

➤ Recognise when you are blaming something outside of yourself for your results, even if your opponent played out of their socks! When you hear the blame coming out of your mouth, in your head (or out loud if you are brave enough) answer the question, "what was my contribution to my result?" Eventually, you will think before the blame comes out and be able to change your response immediately until you are no longer blaming anyone (including yourself) and looking at your own game with self honesty.

➤ Recognise that what you say to yourself will influence your confidence. You sabotage your confidence when you put yourself down and are overly critical and negative towards yourself. Again you need to recognise these self-deprecating comments as you say them and change them around. Recognising them is not as easy as it sounds, since for most players it is an unconscious habit. Changing what you say about yourself is easy. It is a discipline and I would ask you not to get hung up on whether you feel you deserve such positive comments or

whether they are true. Just be disciplined in changing
your current self-talk.

➤ Recognise that your focus is on the outcome rather than
your objectives and bring your focus back to your
performance objectives.

➤ Integrate your mental routines into any points play that
you do in training. Whenever you are practicing to
compete, make sure one of your objectives is to do your
routines on every point and between games and do your
change of ends routines.

The mental game objectives that you follow in training you can
also take into your matches. Again, the important point about
using objectives in matches is that they are there to focus your
attention. So for example by following a mental routine you will
be putting in place the appropriate thinking patterns and
emotional states to play your best tennis. The routine fixes your
mental behaviour, which means you do the same thing every
time. Such mental consistency leads to greater consistency in
your results. The second point that is critical to remember is that
you must avoid the temptation to beat yourself up if you forget
to do an objective during the match. If that happens just become
aware that you are not following it, then pick it up again and
continue.

The main objectives to focus on during a match are tactical
and mental. You would be unlikely to focus your attention on
technical objectives during a competitive match since this would
be a distraction. Sometimes players think that they should be
working out what they are doing wrong but most often this

causes more confusion, tension and frustration than success. If you are not performing as you want to, focus on what you want to achieve and not what you are doing wrong.

Clearly with very young players a coach may give them pointers to go back to if their game is not working well, such as "start hitting to the space". Older players should defer to being more patient and hitting bigger margins when things aren't working, which can feel rather counter intuitive. You need to defer to something that gives you a chance of being competitive, and going for bigger margins does that. Ideally, if you can have a "stock" serve that you can defer to if you need to, such as when under extreme pressure or when your ideal serve isn't working for you, then that can also be very reassuring and keep you in the game longer (although this is more likely for more accomplished players).

Ideally, you would want to be setting your tactical and mental objectives before the match and sticking to them throughout the match. You will also have worked out in your own mind what is the one thing that could throw you off track and identified how you will respond if it happens. Now all you have to do is stick to your plan, which requires you to be mindful in following your objectives rather than being drawn into the scoring and results based approach that you are most used to following.

After the game, evaluate how well you did against the objectives that you set for yourself. Using a percentage score is quite helpful. Also, if you didn't follow your objectives, work out what stopped you? Why did you feel the need to focus on something else? What was the impact of you focusing on something else? And then commit to raising your awareness next time you play so that if a similar thing happens again you will give your objectives even more attention. So, if your objective was to do your routines and then you double fault at the first set point, and you realise that you didn't do your routine, you can evaluate that you need to give even more attention to doing your routines at big points and commit to doing that in the next game. The learning points that come out of each match should be taken forward. If you are taking the same learning points forward and not doing them in the next game then you are blocked in some way. Fear is likely to be a cause which is preventing you from committing to something that is simply a discipline.

Objectives provide a focus and a discipline in the game that enables you to direct your performance and your training. You can use them to measure your progress and recognise whether you are on track to achieve your overall dream goal. Because they provide a structure and discipline some players can find it a difficult process, perhaps because they feel they are not achieving their goals. One thing to remember is that the process of goal setting should be undertaken as a fluid and flexible activity. If you see goals as rigid and in terms of success and failure then you are working in your mind with expectations rather than goals.

GOAL MANAGEMENT

Goals should be managed on a rolling basis rather than simply annually, so I would recommend you sit either with your coach or on your own and regularly evaluate your success relative to your targets. If you are not getting close to your targets then you need to revaluate your goals and or what you are doing to try to get there. Something needs to change if you are not progressing. I worked with a young teenage player whose ratings had not changed in 3 years. This young player was feeling very despondent, and not very successful, but wasn't managing her game in the way I have described above. With a change of emphasis to performance and putting specific targets in place, she was able to feel and see the improvements over a period of time, which led to increased confidence and her competitive performance improved dramatically.

Using goal setting can be very rewarding and I urge you against becoming over zealous with your goal setting. Every goal you set should have a purpose. Setting goals just for the sake of measuring something will not motivate you. It will simply become a process that you could become disillusioned with. Make sure each one of the goals you set for yourself is leading to you improving your performance in the way that you desire. You can even run each of your goals through a mini version of the dream goal setting exercise that you did at the front of this chapter, just to see if you really want it enough. Remember, if you don't want it enough that's fine. Simply be honest with yourself and know that you are choosing. Any other way is an abdication of your responsibility towards yourself and will lead to dissatisfaction. Being honest with yourself feels better, just try it!

37

Your Formula
For Success

Throughout this text I have raised your awareness to the many ways in which your mind works both for and what can appear as against you, the energetic influences on your psyche and the practical realities of achieving peak performance in tennis.

You are only likely to make changes to your mental game within your level of self awareness. You have to overcome fear and resistance to change and build your self-esteem to develop your competitive spirit in a healthy and successful way. If you are unaware of the links between your thinking patterns and your performance outcomes, you will be unlikely to make changes to the way you think. If you undermine yourself you will be unable to build sufficient competitive spirit to get you to your highest potential. You need to learn to embrace change and accept responsibility for your performance.

One of the most disempowering thoughts to hold, which is also not true, is that you have to change your performance before you can change how you think about it. This line of thinking will limit your ability to achieve your peak performance simply because you are saying to yourself that you have to wait until you see great results before you can think differently. Yet, it is the way you are seeing your results that needs to change to allow your performance to shift. You need to recognise that it is the power of your thinking that strongly influences your results because your mind has the power to control your body. Your thinking influences the direction of your energy, so where your attention goes, your energy flows. Your energy and effort drives your outcomes.

In developing your competitive mind and spirit you need to become aware of the potential destructive impact of your ego, as an energetic force that needs you to prove yourself, that has a desire for better results so that you can feel good about yourself and sees what you do in terms of ownership. Overcoming the destructive side of your ego means realising that you are already good enough, that your results are not a measure of your self-worth and that you are playing tennis because of your love for the game and the challenges the game brings for you.

Within the game of tennis, you will be applying your mind and energy to the process of playing tennis to the best of your ability. But this should be done with compassion for yourself. You need to respect yourself enough that you don't feel the need to beat yourself up for errors that you make. You need to learn to accept your outcomes, look for what you can learn from what you did and then make changes in your next challenge. When you put the cause of what happened outside of yourself, you are giving your power over to that thing; you are essentially undermining your self-esteem and your confidence will suffer.

Confidence is one of your greatest allies in the game of tennis and you need to work hard to build it. Every aspect of this book is helping you to build your confidence. One of the biggest influences on your confidence is how you measure yourself and how you measure your success. If you are just looking to your results as a measure of success, then you are missing the point. Your results are always an outcome of what you put into the game and there are other influences on your outcome that you cannot control. You must begin to let go of the results and focus on what you are doing to achieve those results in all dimensions of the game; mental, physical, tactical and technical.

Remember that there are different mindsets for training and competing. The mindset for training is far more focused on getting things right and becoming as skilled as you can. The competing mindset is about trust and acceptance and being present in the game, so very much about playing without analysis. Some will say this is difficult to achieve, but that is only because you are not used to doing it. With practice and especially if you learn through meditation what it is like to have a quiet mind, it is easily possible. But your ego is likely to try to convince you differently, since your ego will feel as if it is losing control when you let go of analysis.

As you continue your journey of tennis development, I am sure that you are now aware that it is a lifestyle. You are building qualities in yourself that will stand you in good stead in your every day life. Recognising that you cannot control things that happen but you can control how you respond to them, puts you back in control of your life. No longer will you respond through instinct and learned childlike behaviours. You will begin to see things through different lenses and feel personally more empowered as you focus your attention on changing that which you can control (you) and let go of trying to control all the things outside of your self, over which you have little or no control.

Each and every one of you will be able to relate to some of what I have said through your own experiences and from what you have seen of others. Some of what I have talked about may resonate with you, other things may not. You will choose to believe what you want to believe and you will become as aware of your game as you wish to. Very simply, you will have your own formula for success and you will want to stick to that. If you choose to become a peak performer then the information I have provided in this book will enable you to get to know yourself and your game better, and you can begin to change the things that aren't helping you. Then you will get the best out of your tennis and your life, and you will achieve personal satisfaction and fulfilment.

As a simple example, some players who experience strong emotions could not even conceive of playing without emotions, those who have high expectations might find it a struggle to let go of them, but the choice as to how far you go is up to you. The only thing you need to be aware of is that for any of your choices there are consequences. Be happy in your choices and accept the consequences. That is the start of being true to yourself and achieving your highest potential.

Enjoy your journey...

What Next?

Congratulations on having started your journey towards achieving peak performance in tennis. This is a continuous process of improvement, as you would expect to do if you were training your forehand. That means you need to continually raise your awareness to what you're doing with your mind and energy. To help you do this and therefore get the best out of your game, I have created a website to complement this book specifically for tennis players, coaches and parents who are committed to achieving peak performance. You can access a wide range of invaluable coaching resources to support your continued development in all the aspects covered in this book and more at:

www.AchievingPeakPerformanceInTennis.com

Specifically you can discover how to:

- ➢ Give yourself effective feedback so you can feel more positive

- ➢ Build your confidence through a programme of activities

- ➢ Start coaching the mental game aspects with your players

- ➢ Learn how to do powerful imagery to enhance your performance

- ➢ Learn more about the practice of meditation and how to relax effectively to improve your power on court

- ➢ Work with Helen directly and/or book her to speak at your event

Glossary

Archetypes. Common thinking patterns, attributes and attitudes that are captured in language symbolically. They are an energetic force that influences our behaviour. The symbols are expressed as the roles people play, such as parent, child, coach, athlete.

Associated. In imagery, seeing something through your own eyes as you would if it were happening now, in the present moment. You will feel more emotion when you look at something from an associated perspective.

Awareness. The process of giving your attention. Noticing things that you did not notice before is the act of raising your awareness. You can raise your awareness to something internally or externally to yourself.

Beliefs. Are the rules around which we construct our reality. We follow our beliefs as if they were true and so they become true for us.

Cause and Effect. The idea that for everything that happens (the effect) in the world, there has to be something(s) that caused it to happen. People often put the causes of things that happen in their life to things outside of themselves rather than looking at what they did that caused the outcome. When you put the cause to something outside of you, you give your power over to that thing.

Chakra. Energy centres within the body, through which your life force energy (chi) flows.

Confidence. A belief in your ability to do something, recognised as a feeling. Often linked with doing something well, so the better I am at something the stronger the feeling of confidence.

Conscious Mind. The thoughts and feelings, which you are aware of right now.

Consequences. The impact of your actions. For every action you take, including your thoughts and feelings, there will be an impact.

Deletion. The process of not noticing something with your senses that is present. It is there but you just don't notice it at the time.

Dissociated. Seeing yourself in the picture. If you recall past events or future imagined images and you are seeing yourself in the picture or movie, then you are looking at it from a dissociated perspective. You will experience less emotion when looking at something from a dissociated perspective.

Distortion. Changing your sensory experience to fit what you want to experience. As when you downplay a compliment that is paid to you.

Ego. A function of the mind. An energetic force that has the desire to label our experiences and define who we are by those experiences. It is our sense of "I", "me" and "mine". Possession is a function of ego. Through ego we become identified with things, thoughts, actions so that we know who we are. It is an illusion of the mind used to define our "self".

Emotion. The feelings we have about our experiences. Sometimes an emotion will be an automatic response to an event because we have learned to link that type of experience to an emotion.

Energy. Your life force. Obtained through the air you breathe, the food you eat and the thoughts you have.

Expectations. Thinking that something "should" happen, often because it has happened before or because on the balance of evidence it should happen. For example a player expecting to beat a player they consider isn't as good as they are.

Fear. A natural human response to a perceived threat. Most often experienced as a feeling, but can be experienced as resistance and mental blocking of things. Fear can be experienced as extreme or mild.

Fight or Flight Response. Your natural human physiological response to something that threatens you. Sets off your sympathetic nervous system, which prepares you to either fight or run. Threats can be experienced as thoughts as well as physically.

Filters. The method we use to narrow down what we give our attention to in order to create our internal representation of our experience e.g. beliefs, values, memories, language etc.

Generalisation. The process of linking your interpretation of a single experience to all experiences of the same type. For example, hitting one or two poor serves becomes generalised by the player when they say that they are serving poorly. The poor serves are generalised to all their serves.

Imagery. The act of using your creative imagination, through your senses and in your mind, to imagine anything you choose. Worries are imagery. Seeing yourself being successful is also imagery.

Instinctive Response. Your natural or first response that happens without your conscious awareness. It is an automatic response, such as in the fight or flight response, or learned response as in your anger at hitting the ball in the net. You can learn to change your instinctive responses.

Intention. Your mentally planned actions. If you intend to focus on your serve, that is your planned action. There will be a motivation or purpose to your intention.

Law of Attraction. The concept that we attract what comes to us because of how we direct our thoughts, feelings and actions. We direct good and bad things because we focus our attention ineffectively on what we don't want to happen rather than on what we do want to happen.

Light. In the context of archetypes, the light is that of which we are aware. It tends to be a positive attribute with benefits to self and others.

Like Attracts Like. Taken from the Law of Attraction, the idea that from an energetic perspective, we attract that which is like ourselves.

Meridian. The route and system by which energy (chi) travels around our body. Meridian lines run up and down our body.

Mind. Our conscious and unconscious processing of our experiences as experienced in our head and body.

NLP. Neuro-Linguistic Programming is the art and science of how we use our mind to make sense of our experiences. How we communicate with ourselves and with others. It is often described as the user manual to your mind.

Outcome. The end result of an action.

Peak Performance. Achieving your highest standard of performance on a consistent basis.

Perception. How we make sense of the world through our senses. It is linked to our awareness since we can only be as aware as we are open to the experience of our senses.

Perception is Projection. The concept that what we experience on the outside of us is a projection from within us. Since we cannot experience the world directly, we can only experience it through our senses, anything we project will be based upon our filtered interpretation. Therefore our perception is actually a projection from within us.

Perfectionism. The concept of being perfect where anything less is not acceptable and considered a failure. Getting things right and achieving a standard that keeps shifting higher and higher, such that you are never satisfied.

Performance. The art of delivering what you have been trained to do in a competitive arena or the art of behaving in a particular way to get the best out of yourself, as in the training arena.

Performance Objectives. Setting tasks for yourself that you give your attention to that are designed to drive the behaviour you want, whether mental, tactical, physical or technical.

Peripheral Vision. The act of broadening your visual field to become aware of everything that lies at the external edges of your vision. The opposite is foveal vision and this is the act of focusing in a narrow way on something very specific.

Perspective. Your take on something. Your view, your appreciation, your understanding. Also refers to other's views.

Physiology. Your body's internal and external response to everything, including your thoughts and feelings and things that happen outside of you.

Process of Tennis. Those aspects of your tennis that form the ingredients that lead to your outcomes. The process would be carrying out the objectives you set for yourself, doing your routines, controlling your emotional state, dealing with errors, managing pressure, etc.

Psyche. Your self and your soul. It is what makes you, you.

Responsibility. The act of being accountable for your game rather than blaming other things for what happens.

Self-Esteem. Your internal feeling of self-worth. Built by being true to yourself and developing a strong internal reference system, rather than following others against your will.

Self-Talk. The thoughts you experience in your head, sometimes experienced as an inner voice.

Shadow. In the context of archetypes is that part of ourselves of which we are unaware. Often negatively associated in that it can be damaging to your development and that of others.

Shadowing. The act of physically going through the motions of a shot without the ball. As if miming.

Spirit. That sense of personal strength and determination that comes from deep within you. A sense of faith in yourself. An energy that surrounds you and is within you.

Tanking. The act of giving up in the game, usually when you are losing. Tanking can happen physically and mentally.

Unconscious Mind. The part of your mind that stores everything you have ever experienced. The part of your mind of which you can be mostly unaware. Raising awareness requires that you make conscious that which you do unconsciously. Your unconscious mind drives instinctive behaviours and natural human processes, such as breathing and your heart beating.

Values. Are those things which are important to you. Your values provide your energy and motivation to take action. They are also the way in which you evaluate your success.

Zone. Is that state of higher functioning, where there is an absence of thought and a total engagement in the task. There are many attributes of the zone, one of which is a trance like state.

Index

About the Author

Helen Emms has coached and inspired thousands of people throughout the UK to unleash their potential. From her experiences in the Army, coaching sports teams and training soldiers to cope in the highest pressure situations through to her role in Industry, developing high performing teams, Helen knows how to tap into each person's inner motivation for success. Her own insatiable appetite for learning and passion for discovering new ways to work with her clients has led Helen to achieve the highest level of qualification and practical experience as a Psychologist, Clinical Hypnotherapist, Certified Trainer of NLP, EFT Practitioner, Reiki Master and Peak Performance Coach. Helen is now currently supporting one of the UK's top Tennis Academies and works with coaches, players and their parents to achieve peak performance in tennis.

If you would like more information about how Helen will help you achieve your best in tennis or any other sport, please visit her website at www.spiritinsport.co.uk.

Lightning Source UK Ltd.
Milton Keynes UK
11 December 2009

147359UK00001B/138/P